Tim Brown is one of the finest Christian men I have ever met. Tim is not only a great teacher of golf, but his passion and love for Christ and the word of God go to the very core of who he is and how he has raised his family.

— Rev. Larry Smith,
TH.D Theology

Several years ago, I joined a Bible study run by Tim Brown. I was a newly-minded Christian struggling to incorporate faith into my daily life. Tim was not only a teacher by word, but most importantly by example. He not only taught the Word but lived it in his daily life.

Being able to hear him teach and watch him live has helped me transform my life over time in a way that has made what could have been temporary into a way of living life every day for the rest of my days. I have the most beautiful relationship with my Father, the creator of all things. I can recognize how He shows up in my life all day, every day.

Most importantly, Tim has taught me that my struggles are an opportunity to draw closer to God each moment of every day by moving from a flesh-driven place to a Spirit-driven heart for God. I am the luckiest of people to be taught by one who lives the Word of God.

— Alita Miller

the sacred seven

Seven Imperatives to Manifest
Your Kingdom Potential

TIM BROWN

The Sacred Seven: Seven Imperatives to Manifest Your Kingdom Potential

Trilogy Christian Publishers
A Wholly Owned Subsidiary of Trinity Broadcasting Network
2442 Michelle Drive Tustin, CA 92780

Copyright © 2022 by Tim Brown

Scripture quotations marked ESV are taken from the ESV® Bible (The Holy Bible, English Standard Version®), copyright © 2001 by Crossway Bibles, a publishing ministry of Good News Publishers. Used by permission. All rights reserved.

Scripture quotations marked NIV are taken from the Holy Bible, New International Version®, NIV®. Copyright © 1973, 1978, 1984, 2011 by Biblica, Inc.™ Used by permission of Zondervan. All rights reserved worldwide. www.zondervan.com. The "NIV" and "New International Version" are trademarks registered in the United States Patent and Trademark Office by Biblica, Inc.™

Scripture quotations marked NLT are taken from the Holy Bible, New Living Translation, copyright © 1996, 2004, 2015 by Tyndale House Foundation. Used by permission of Tyndale House Publishers, Inc., Carol Stream, Illinois 60188. All rights reserved.

Scripture quotations marked TLB are taken from The Living Bible copyright © 1971. Used by permission of Tyndale House Publishers, a Division of Tyndale House Ministries, Carol Stream, Illinois 60188.

Scripture quotations marked TPT are from The Passion Translation®. Copyright © 2017, 2018 by Passion & Fire Ministries, Inc. Used by permission. All rights reserved. ThePassionTranslation.com.

Scripture quotations marked NKJV are taken from the New King James Version®. Copyright © 1982 by Thomas Nelson. Used by permission. All rights reserved.

Scripture quotations marked KJV are taken from the King James Version of the Bible. Public domain.

No part of this book may be reproduced, stored in a retrieval system, or transmitted by any means without written permission from the author. All rights reserved. Printed in the USA.
Rights Department, 2442 Michelle Drive, Tustin, CA 92780.

Trilogy Christian Publishing/TBN and colophon are trademarks of Trinity Broadcasting Network. For information about special discounts for bulk purchases, please contact Trilogy Christian Publishing.

Trilogy Disclaimer: The views and content expressed in this book are those of the author and may not necessarily reflect the views and doctrine of Trilogy Christian Publishing or the Trinity Broadcasting Network.

Manufactured in the United States of America
10 9 8 7 6 5 4 3 2 1
Library of Congress Cataloging-in-Publication Data is available.

ISBN: 978-1-63769-700-9
E-ISBN: 978-1-63769-701-6

DEDICATION

*This book is dedicated to my wife Kimberly
and my three incredible children.*

*Kim, my beautiful wife,
thank you for never giving up on me.
Thank you for being my partner in spirit and in life.*

*To my children,
Joshua, Sarah, and Timothy,
in whom I am well pleased.
God has great things for you;
go and walk them out.
I love you.*

For this cause we also, since the day we heard it,
do not cease to pray for you, and to desire that ye
might be filled with the knowledge of his will in all
wisdom and spiritual understanding;

That ye might walk worthy of the Lord unto
all pleasing, being fruitful in every good work, and
increasing in the knowledge of God.

— Colossians 1:9-10, KJV

ACKNOWLEDGMENTS

I wish to offer a special word of gratitude to the people who made the writing possible and have impacted my life enormously.

Spiritual

Kurt Cottrell, thank you, Sir.

Thank you, Bob Byers, Kimo Bethea, and Pastor Jim Croft, for starting it all.

Pastor Larry and Sharon Smith for teaching me the power of prayer and having the greatest impact on my life as a father and husband. None of this would have happened without "Resurrection Fellowship" and the Smiths. Moreover, thank you for introducing Kim and me to the "muffuletta."

Pastor Michael Millé and Pastor Elaine Millé for teaching me everything, especially God's Word like only you can. Thank you for showing me that we all can experience revelation, mentorship, discipleship, and live a life of faith people would wish to emulate.

Pastor Greg and Kristi Hollis, thank you for your work, obedience, impacting my children, and your labor of love at the Power Place.

Family

To my mother, I love you Mom!

To my brothers, Dave and Brian, and to my sister Jacqueline. I love you and thank you for contributing to who I am today.

vii

The Porters, Browns, Beckhardts, Poetas, I love you all.

A special thanks to the best stepmom a guy could have—thank you, Cindy Lou. I love you.

To Jimmy Goss, love you and thank you for all you do.

Friends

Mike Nealy, Steve, and Michelle Conte, I am forever indebted to you three and your families.

Wayne King and Mrs. Fran, I love you and thank you for being such an integral part of my life.

Mike Laplante and family.

Chris Clewes, my man.

To my small group, thank you for letting me pour out the Word to you. Trust me; I have gleaned more from you.

To my NOLA peeps, you have my heart.

Professionally

Adrian March, for introducing me to golf.

Bob Crissy, for giving me my first golf lesson.

Marty Martinez for hiring me at St. Andrews.

John and Joan Lubin for giving me the opportunity to start my career.

Martin Hall, what can I say, my friend? Words cannot express how grateful I truly am. You modeled what it would take to be a successful teacher, provider, and person.

Chuck Winstead, I learned so much about life, people, and golf from you. You are so very responsible for any success that I have had as a coach and a human. Thank you.

TABLE OF CONTENTS

Dedication v
Acknowledgments vii

Introduction: The Car Ride 11
Chapter 1. The First Imperative: The Progenitor 17
Chapter 2. The Second Imperative: The Perspective 31
Chapter 3. The Third Imperative: The Progress 47
Chapter 4. The Fourth Imperative: The Paradigm 67
Chapter 5. The Fifth Imperative: The Profession. 83
Chapter 6. The Sixth Imperative: The Perdition 99
Chapter 7. The Seventh Imperative: The Pivot 105

Notes and Reference 115

INTRODUCTION

The Car Ride

He has declared that he will set you in praise, fame
and honor HIGH ABOVE all the nations he has
made and that you will be a people holy to the Lord
your God, as he promised.

— Deuteronomy 26:19, NIV

In the early 2000s, I took a job teaching golf full time at the
beautiful English Turn Golf and Country Club on the West
Bank of New Orleans. My wife and I moved to New Orleans
in December of 1999 and spent the coming years falling more in
love with the people, the culture, and of course, the food.

After a few short years attending a local church, we were
approached regarding a high school-aged Sunday school class
needing leaders. As one would imagine for that age bracket,
Sunday school can be a tough sell. However, my wife and I
embraced the challenge. She also thought it would be a great
experience, especially since our kids were young, and it would be
a practice round for us as parents.

My next step was to arrange a meeting with the education
department leader, Pastor Bob Koeling. Pastor Koeling was not
only an experienced minister, but he held multiple degrees in
teaching. As a golf pro at a private club, Monday was my day off,
and this one Monday morning meeting would be an important
one for my family and me.

The idea was to pick his brain on how we could turn this
small group around and help these kids grow in Christ. Pastor K

gave me two pieces of advice. First, he told me that it's not about the teaching techniques; rather, it is about the kids—"Relationships are the key, Tim. If they don't trust you, they will not confide in you. Get to know them and let them see that you care." Second, he instructed me to give them a *"specific objective"* every time my wife and I teach. I interpreted that as a warning not to over-train but instead teach one element the kids could quickly learn and implement. Although I used a similar approach in my golf instruction, I loved how he phrased it. The wording was straightforward: *specific objective*. After our Monday sit-down, I think I used that phrase in almost every Sunday school class and golf lesson from that day forward.

On the first day of Sunday school, Kim and I had only three kids in attendance. Within a few short months, we proceeded to outgrow the room twice. God did a remarkable thing in that high school group, not only for the kids but for my wife and me as well—an incredible time for all parties.

Years later, when my kids were of high school age, we had relocated as a family and lived in a different state, attended a new church, and worked at a new golf facility. One day, I needed some help picking up a few things from the teaching studio. So, I grabbed my two boys and proceeded to drive to the golf center.

As was my custom, I used the family car rides as opportunities to speak into their lives. There was no escaping sixty-five miles-per-hour down the highway; I had them in a secure environment. Seizing the moment to pour into them again, I asked them if they had ever heard the term *trophic dynamics*. My younger son was in the back seat, shaking his head 'no' as I glanced up in the rearview.

My oldest son, however, piped up and said, "I haven't heard that term, but I believe it has something to do with the food chain."

I was stoked he had figured that out. I asked him how he knew, and he explained how he understood the meanings of the roots of the words; that dynamic is linked to movement, and trophic comes from troph, which is Greek for food.[1]

"That's right," I said, "Trophic dynamics is a fancy term for the food chain." Moreover, according to Colin Dunn, "trophic levels are used to describe the positions of different organisms in a given ecosystem, and within that system, there exists a keystone species called *apex predators.*"[2]

By this time on the ride, I was in full preaching mode. I continued, informing the trapped youngsters about the vital connection between God's purpose for their lives and this ecological occurrence. I communicated that Christians are the earth's *keystone species* and share similar qualifying characteristics.

First, I told them how apex predators reside at the top of the food chain, and so do God's redeemed; for our Lord qualified us to be "the head and not the tail" (Deuteronomy 28:13, NKJV). Second, I made them aware that apex predators have no natural predators. The Christian equivalent of having no natural predators is the fact that "no weapon formed shall succeed" (Isaiah 54:17, NLT). My final point emphasized that apex predators play a *crucial role* in the overall health and wellbeing of the ecosystem in which they reside, and so should we.

My message was poignant, telling them that in Christ, they never have to struggle with finding purpose or the wonder about the "meaning of life." God has already given them a *specific objective* that just so happens to be the most important calling in the world: to play the role of the apex performer in this ecosystem called earth.

The Cascade

Brothers and sisters, we need to grasp the fact that we are responsible for the environment God gives us. Being a father, a mother, a teacher, an entertainer, an athlete, a craftsman, we all have people and areas where God planted us. When we don't pursue the calling to rise, things erode quickly. In trophic dynamics, there is a phenomenon called a *cascade*. Cascades occur when the *keystone species* is removed from the ecosystem.[3] The consequence is an outbreak at the lower level, creating an imbalance.

In my experience as a Christian for more than twenty-five years, a Sunday school teacher, a men's group leader, and a participant in a church plant, I have seen so many people - myself included - make the mistake of waiting for God to give them their purpose. Time and time again, I hear people utter this phrase: "I know God saved me for a reason, and I know I have a purpose; I just don't know what it is." Well, I do, and I believe He has already given us our purpose.

> "All who are mine belong to you, and you have given
> them to me, so they bring me glory."
>
> — John 17:10 (NLT)

Our purpose, now privy to the light of the King, is to cultivate a deep love relationship with our God and relentlessly pursue our kingdom potential. Performing His Word and His will shall result in a life's witness so profound it reflects Christ and makes a critical contribution to our area of influence. Without us, living as God has ordained, our ecosystem and its inhabitants are in an unending state of decay.

Now What

Hopefully, I have your attention? But my real objective is to affect your intention. You may be wondering, "What do we do now?" Well, I think I have an answer. Integrate.

I have been coaching professionally for more than twenty-seven years, and I can tell you the difference between an effective coach and an ineffective coach comes down to what the student does when the coach is not around. That is why I wrote the book. This manual is designed for integration. Integrating God's principles to reach our potential, so He gets glorified, and people are impacted.

Therefore, I am offering seven imperatives for you to assimilate. These SACRED SEVEN skills will assist your journey. Implement these kingdom imperatives immediately, and there will be no doubt that you will achieve a new level of potential, purpose, and performance.

CHAPTER 1

The First Imperative: The Progenitor

My Garden Experience

For my people have committed two evils; they
have forsaken me the fountain of living waters, and
hewed them out cisterns, broken cisterns, that can
hold no water.

— Jeremiah 2:13, KJV

Jeremiah 2:13 is a scripture that changed my life. I first discovered it in 2001, and I've gleaned so much from it over the years; it is one of those scriptures you never forget. My pastor in Louisiana calls these types of scriptures *gateway* scriptures because they stick with you for a lifetime, impact you in ways you would have never imagined, and become an entrance to another level. I hope it will become a gateway for you as well.

My wife and I purchased our first home in 2001. Like most men, I think I liked the outside of the house more than the inside. There was a privacy fence, a very long driveway, a fishpond, and the yard was extravagantly landscaped—all types of different trees, bushes, and foliage. In the middle of that fishpond was a beautiful flowing fountain. The flow and the sound of the pond were soothing.

At the time of our settlement, we moved into our new home, both excited and nervous. After a few hectic days, as we nestled in, I finally went out to the backyard to check out the lush scenery and foliage, looking for some peace and quiet. But something was missing. It was too quiet; something was wrong. Then I noticed the fountain was gone. They left some of the fish in the pond but took the fountain.

I was puzzled; I could not understand why someone would remove the fountain and leave the fish and other living organisms in that state. Life for them obviously can't function very long, and indeed, death was imminent. I put fresh water from the hose in the pond then told myself I must investigate a replacement "when I get some time."

One thing led to the next, and with everything going on between moving and working, all with three young children, I became so busy that I put the pond on the back burner. I had neglected to restore the fountain, and my procrastination would cost me dearly.

Foregoing the fountain started a chain reaction of unstable events. I am sure you can imagine; we all know what happens when the source is removed—the water lies still. The next time I found myself in the backyard, I encountered a foul stench. My oasis was not as *appealing* as it once was. It *was no longer attractive* because the water started to turn from clean to toxic. Unfortunately, because of my ignorance, I had to maintain the basin constantly. The pond became quite *labor-intensive*, it needed constant attending. I had to work continuously, draining and cleaning, just to place more water back in the cistern.

Without the flow from the fountain, I had to *replenish it from an artificial source.* It was an uphill struggle, all for naught, running around the same mountain working in vain to keep what little I had left in the pond. Even more devastating was my decision to forsake the fountain, creating an environment that *could not sustain life* in that ecosystem. Unfortunately, that is the end game when the progenitor is ignored.

"A progenitor is defined as a person or thing that first indicates a direction, originates something, or serves as a model; predecessor; precursor."[4]

The Source

Yet for us there is only one God—the Father. He
is the source of all things, and our lives are lived for
him. And there is one Lord, Jesus, the Anointed
One, through whom we and all things exist.

—1 Corinthians 8:6, TPT

There is much we could unearth from my garden account, but I am hopeful you have already picked up on what I have put down. I have specific reasons for recanting my story, reasons which are essential to us living a life that functions in the way and the will of Jesus. To avoid making the same mistake that I had made, I would ask all to think about the upcoming details that will most definitely shape your stride as a disciple.

God Is Relational

Royalty is my identity; Servanthood is my
assignment; Intimacy with God is my life source.[5]

—Bill Johnson

The first of these reasons is obvious. We can't live without water. Make no mistake about it; there can be no discussion of potential and destiny without a relationship with God. It's all about Him. It always has been and will be. Our life's mission should be couched in cultivating union with Father.

Relationship is central to God's very nature. Early on, God said, "Let Us make man." (Genesis 1:26) In uttering that specific phrase, He gave us a clue into His design and structure. Although He is one God, He has a *relationship* among the other in the Trinity—Father, Son, and Holy Ghost. When God made us, we too were imprinted with a desire to relate, first and foremost, to Him. For we are intended *for intimacy and created for impact*.

During my personal garden experience, the Lord made it very clear that procrastinating in restoring the fountain was akin to me not prioritizing time with Him through prayer or reading His Word. That did not mean I wasn't a Christian anymore or that God did not love me. No, indeed. It did mean that I was choosing the busyness of life over my time with Him. As a result, I naturally kicked into doing work *without* the incredible benefit of God's direct and personal interaction. Communion with Him is a primary message of the Bible. "For God so loved"[6] that He sent His Son to be torn. The veil now opened; we have complete and unfettered access to the fountain. My brothers and sisters, eternal life is to know the progenitor.

A Tale of Two Systems

The second reason for sharing this experience may not be so apparent. I refer to this point as "a tale of two systems."

As you can imagine, springs in those days were not always easy to find. Therefore, it was necessary to hew out cisterns/wells as storage. In addition, the more people, the demand increased, so they dug basins from the stone to catch the rain. That doesn't sound too good. Water from runoff in a dry, dusty desert region was not too enticing.

Taking a closer look revealed other alarming flaws and weaknesses of cistern use. Because cisterns were essentially holding tanks dug from stone, the supply was naturally limited and temporary. As a result, life's source was restrained by size, evaporation, and seepage from the cracks and crevasses in the porous rock. Without the fountain to bring the flow, the water had to be *gathered, retrieved, and worked.* To survive, people *would repeatedly dig* and *travail to quench their thirst.*

I hope you got that point because we often do the same when neglecting the fountain.

My objective for us, as believers, is to realize we are looking at a verse that describes two *completely different systems* with completely different characteristics and consequences. There is an endless, pure surplus in one system, and the other system, as you can imagine from my story, is lacking and incredibly laborious. One system is light, and the other system is darkness. One system we call the kingdom, and the other the cosmos. One approach is built by divine design, and the other is artificial and demonically arranged. In one system, you have access to surplus from a pristine source, Christ himself; the other requires constant sweat from the brow, under the supervision of a pharaoh, the taskmaster, who comes to enslave.

This spiritual dichotomy is fundamental throughout the entirety of both testaments. In the old, there were two trees in the garden, two mountains to live on, and two houses to dwell in. Subsequently, the New Testament offers us two realms from which we can reside. "The realm of the flesh and the realm of the Spirit" as referenced in Romans 8:19 (NIV).

All the examples are symbolic of the two choices God has presented to us. One faith, the other flawed. A choice between life or death, blessing or curse, worry or worship, supply or lack, weak or strong, light, and dark—and in this case, *drink from the fountain or dig on our own.*

As a Spirit-empowered Christian, I believe in work. I feel it is our duty to dig a well. We should want to dig a well large enough to invite others to drink. However, *digging our own well apart from the Holy Spirit's* guidance cannot provide adequate supply for ourselves, let alone anyone else. Conscious or unconscious, making decisions to move away from the life-sustaining flow of the Father will automatically thrust us into a faulty, broken cistern. A cistern/system with devastating consequences and a life that lacks eternal contribution.

Kingdom Cause and Effect

So you must remain in life-union with me, [a] for
I remain in life-union with you. For as a branch
severed from the vine will not bear fruit, so your life
will be fruitless unless you live your life intimately
joined to mine.

— John 15:4, The Passion Translation

Now to my third point: I call it Kingdom Cause and Effect.

Cause and effect are concepts with which I am incredibly familiar. I use them every day; you could say it's how I make a living.

You see, my ability to understand and correctly discern the difference between cause and effect is at the forefront of my profession. Differentiating between the two is a skill I rely on heavily. It is a strength in my teaching, and it has helped me assist many.

Let me explain. When coaching, I first look at the flight of the ball. This is a critical step, for the game of golf is a ball control sport. Here is the cool part: by watching the flight, I know exactly how the instrument was applied. My diagnosis starts with the flight/fruit. If I get that part wrong, both the student and I waste time, and frustration will result. I will probably get

22   *The Sacred Seven*

fired, and worse, the player will go in *a different direction, searching for truth.*

A similar scenario is true for us as Christians. That is why I believe our ability to recognize cause and effect is paramount to our potential. Just as the ball flight in golf tells us how the golf instrument was applied, our fruit demonstrates how we have used His instrument, the WORD. Because of the incredible implications of God's Word in our lives, we can't afford a misdiagnosis. God is good, patient, and kind. He is the God of second chances. However, moving away from the knowledge and obedience of our Lord's teaching takes further from the actual fix, Christ.

In NOLA, my cistern had no source. So, what was the effect? The need to constantly tend and toil in vain. Now I must find a way to replenish. No wonder the woman at the well had five husbands and still had to visit repeatedly.

Folks, we can't replace the love of God. We cannot receive our true purpose and identity, disconnected from the Progenitor. Furthermore, without the purposeful prioritizing of His presence, there is less intimate communication from Spirit to spirit. Ignoring the Master equals less supernatural living water to be accessed. As we leave the ideal source of supply, we limit our capacity and potential by retrieving and relying on the natural mind. The classic carnal default is to override the loss of Revelation with polluted human reason and logic.

We can't survive independently of the Progenitor, let alone develop. Even entire churches can be infiltrated and are not exempt from passing on the spring. If you want a biblical precedent, observe Paul Younggi Cho's evaluation of the church of Ephesus in the book of Revelation:

The church at Ephesus was privileged among all the churches because it was blessed with the best of the day's pastors. It was successively pastored by the Apostle Paul, Apollos, Timothy, and the Apostle John. It was, therefore, the most trained in the scriptures and doctrinally orthodox. But as the church greatly expanded thanks to its firm standing on the word of God, it changed into an organization and became systemized. Naturally, little by little, its first love began to wane and grow cold. Prayer and praise ceased too, and the worship service leaned towards form and ritual.[7]

Compensations

O Lord, I know that the way of man is not in himself; it is not in man who walks to direct his steps.

— Jeremiah 10:23

Just like in the golf swing, compensation must now be employed. As we layer mistake upon mistake, trying everything and desperately searching for answers, we move away from optimal alignments and techniques. Well, I'm here to tell you the same thing happens in our lives; I've seen it time and time again. Oh, and by the way, I've made the same mistake a few times myself. In essence, as people, we start seeking love in all the wrong places. Why? Our manufactured cisterns are flawed and fractured, and naturally require constant effort to maintain.

Compensation can be defined as:

the process of concealing or offsetting a psychological difficulty by developing in another direction. A mechanism by which an individual attempts to make up for some real or imagined deficiency of personality or behavior by developing or stressing another aspect of the personality or by substituting a different form of behavior.[8]

— Dictonary.com

There is no substitute for Him or His presence; therefore, we find ourselves on the road to futility. Our most significant loss is our relationship with the Progenitor and His life-giving hydration. Without it, you will never be satisfied; you will never improve, and worse, you may quit altogether. All the problems in humans can be traced to people trying to offset the one determinant deficiency, not knowing Christ.

You were created with God's purpose in mind. Until you discover his will and follow through on it, there will always be a hole in your soul.[9]

— Andy Stanley

Bypassing the presence and supernatural provision takes us farther and farther from the trustworthy source. A perpetual state of adjustments now becomes the new normal. Fleeting attempts at replacement begin, going around the mountain drawing from the tainted wells, teeming with unwholesome matter. Addictions, divorce, anger, religion, even unbalanced drive are all drinks we resort to attempting to quench the thirst; these drinks are not fit for consumption. Religion? Yes, the water is purest close to the spring. Religion without relationships is consuming water well downstream.

God has decided what you could be and should
be. And through Christ, he has brought about
and continues to bring about changes in you in
accordance with his picture of what you could and
should be. But his vision for you is not complete
simply because God has the vision. It has to be
made into a reality. So, you have a crucial part in it.[10]

— Andy Stanley

Has science or the world system ever sufficiently addressed
one's purpose and destiny? Nope, they haven't; when God is
omitted it is the wrong well. Subsequently, there is no ability to
quench the thirst without the spiritual stimulus from the Progenitor Himself.

No one can escape the causality between knowing Him and
not knowing Him. The lack of true intimacy is the thirst that
drives us toward something other than God.

Apex performers were never intended to work, live, or dwell
disconnected from the Progenitor.

Derek Prince states, "independence being something that
God never wanted for us." [11]

Don't lose sight of the fact that the Father is big into cause
and effect. It's just so fascinating, especially as a coach, to see
how His message to Jeremiah was so simple and yet so insightful. God is so succinct. Instead of listing every sin or mistake,
He proceeds directly to the real issues: two causes, not seventeen, only two. In doing so, He accurately identified the primary issues, pointing out not only the problem His kids were
having (speaking to Judah through Jeremiah in context) but all
of humanity.

Misguided Mastery

In Genesis 1:28 (NKJV) it says, "and God bless them, and God said unto them, be fruitful and multiply, and replenish the Earth, and subdue it: have dominion over the fish of the sea, and over the fowl of the air, and over every living thing that moveth upon the Earth."

When God created man, He told His creation to "subdue and to have dominion" (Genesis 1:28, NKJV), but He never intended that dominion be independent of Him. God never intended mastery without the Master. That is why I do not teach self-mastery. I advocate renewing our thoughts from the well of the Master's mind. "And no one puts new wine into old wineskins. For the old skins would burst from the pressure, spilling the wine and ruining the skins" (Matt 9:17a, NLT).

This world is built on talent, self-indulgence, looks, competition, and survival of the fittest. This is knowledge gathered apart from God's governance. My advice is to immediately flee that system. There is no other supply except Christ.

> "I am the sprouting vine and you're my branches. As you live in union with me as your source, fruitfulness will stream from within you—but when you live separated from me you are powerless. If a person is separated from me, he is discarded; such branches are gathered up and thrown into the fire to be burned. But if you live in life-union with me and if my words live powerfully within you—then you can ask whatever you desire, and it will be done. When your lives bear abundant fruit, you demonstrate that you are my mature disciples who glorify my Father.

"I love each of you with the same love that the
Father loves me. You must continually let my love
nourish your hearts."

— John 15:5-9, The Passion Translation

The Prodigal Son

and not many days after the younger son gathered
all together, journeyed to a far country, and there he
wasted his possession with prodigal living. but when
he had spent it all, there arose a severe famine in the
land, and he began to be in want, then he went and
joined himself to a citizen of that country, and he
sent him into his field to feed swine.

— Luke 15:13 – 15 (NKJV)

An excellent New Testament picture of systems can be seen
in the life of the prodigal son. In this most popular story, the
youngest, and likely the most immature, decides he wants his
independence. He asks for his inheritance and jets from his
father's house. He leaves the presence, the house of blessing, to
live in the world system.

Matthew Henry says, "a sinful state is a state of departure
and distance from God." [12]

Next, he journeys to a faraway country. He leaves the safety,
love, and provision of his father's kingdom and becomes subject
to the governing entities of that foreign land.

The prodigal now compounds his error. When the famine
hit and no supply was available, instead of returning to the father
immediately, he joined himself to a foreign lord to become a

tenant of a strange system. The word *joined* is essential because, in Greek, it means "to glue."[13] For me, it is a simple message; the longer we spend time in that land, the more we begin to adhere to its laws and customs, thereby accumulating ungodly values. The young son submitted himself to a foreign authority.

From Prodigal to Performer

Now we see the power of true repentance. Pastor Bob Koeling, who I mentioned earlier in the book, spoke of the prodigal's moment of "coming to himself" this way, *"it's never the desperation you're in, but the decisions you make."*[14] If you are reading this and find yourself joined to a foreign land, run back to Father God right now.

Too much time spent in the far country eventually leads to desperate times. *The demonic realm will leave you devoid, depleted, deprived, and disrobed.*

Life in the world system is simply more difficult. The "wages of sin" (Romans 6:23, KJV) are taxing on the human soul and body. Desperation and duress will defile your capacity to decide. Emotions unchecked produce chemicals in the mind and body, making our ability to think clearly more difficult. Digging in desperation tends to push people toward doing bad things. God is not mad at you, nor is He punishing you; it is the system you chose.

CHAPTER 2

The Second Imperative: The Perspective

But the godly shall flourish like palm trees and grow tall as the cedars of Lebanon.

— Psalm 92:12, TLB

Perspective Is Paramount

As a coach, I always consider two things before recommending an intervention: first, I ask myself, "What is the earliest mistake the client is making?" Second, I pursue the *lead domino*. "The lead domino is the task that, when completed, will make all the other tasks easier.[15]"

Based on years of experience teaching, thousands of lessons, and countless hours on the range, I believe that one's perspective is the lead domino. Simply, *how you view, is how you do*. It all starts with perspective.

Perspective Defined

Perspective is the way you view something. It is your vantage point, outlook, your worldview, and your life philosophy. Our cultural context and viewpoints, in combination with the feelings produced become the foundation of our actions. Whether or not we recognize it, our life views drive our decisions.

Since beliefs beget behaviors, we believers should constantly examine and evaluate our perspective as it produces practices, particularly when it comes to faith. Suggesting change to behavior without first examining and diagnosing what is driving that behavior is highly inefficient and often leads to frustration and failure.

Our willingness to adopt an eternal perspective will have the greatest influence on reaching our destiny and potential. After all, high-performance results require a high-performance thought life, with none higher than our Lord's. Problems arise from adopting thought patterns that are not in unison with God's Word; instead, they are grounded in the world system. As a result, we act accordingly and walk out a path moving aside from the Father of Heaven and closer to the father of lies.

Setting the Captive Free

There is no doubt that Jesus is acutely attuned to the importance and power of perspective. A few years back, I studied the gospels one chapter at a time. Each day I took one chapter and really looked to see how Jesus went about His Father's business. In that time, I noticed something very significant—it was very apparent that Christ "set the captive free" using three distinct methods:

- First, He healed the sick. Christ spent much of His time healing infirmities.
- Second, He dealt with the demonic. No one who reads the gospels can deny that much of His ministry had to do with handling the demonic realm. We will handle that issue later in the book.
- The third strategy was how Jesus would pound away at perspective.

A *renewed mind* (perspective) is a significant point of emphasis in the scripture. I could see how Christ set the people free by presenting them with a different belief system based on revelation. For example, the words "verily, I say unto you"[16] are used more than sixty times in the four gospels. I believe His motive in doing so was to *erase and replace* their current "operating system" riddled with condemnation, frustration, and bondage brought about by the religious establishment.

In the famous Sermon on the Mount, Jesus specifically targeted perspective. Repeatedly, He is contrasting worldly thinking from the kingdom's point of view. For instance, in the book of Matthew, He states the following:

> [17] Think not that I am come to destroy the law, or the prophets: I am not come to destroy, but to fulfil.
> [18] For verily I say unto you, Till heaven and earth pass, one jot or one tittle shall in no wise pass from the law, till all be fulfilled.
>
> — Matthew 5:17-18, KJV

Christ is campaigning for an exchange at the highest level. He reveals the false narrative they have embraced and renewed their frame of reference.

Jesus and Pilate

In my opinion, one of the most outstanding examples of perspective driving behavior is the account of Jesus' interaction with Pontius Pilot. The revelation at this moment is mind-blowing. I've never heard anyone preach or teach on this scripture in this manner, so I hope it has as much impact on you as it did me.

Then Pilate went back into his headquarters and called for Jesus to be brought to him. "Are you the king of the Jews?" he asked him.

Jesus replied, "Is this your own question, or did others tell you about me?"

"Am I a Jew?" Pilate retorted. "Your own people and their leading priests brought you to me for trial. Why? What have you done?"

Jesus answered, "My Kingdom is not an earthly kingdom. If it were, my followers would fight to keep me from being handed over to the Jewish leaders. But my Kingdom is not of this world."

— John 18:33-36, NLT

In this incredible interaction, Jesus was saying, "If I thought the way you thought, if I had your perspective, there would be a brawl in the streets right now." Instead, Christ demonstrated an entirely supernatural action because He had a completely different internal compass. If our Lord had taken a humanistic approach to His decision-making, there would have been bloodshed. However, since He is using an eternal belief system, based in the heavenly realm, a different choice was made, a choice that He knew would lead Him right to the cross. A different reaction would have brought on catastrophic consequences for humans. Regardless of circumstance, despite knowing full well what was in store for Him, Jesus maintained an eternal mindset—therefore, performing His Father's will, and He did it for us.

Before Christ

My outlook on who Jesus is has changed throughout my more than twenty-five years of knowing and pursuing Him. Therefore, my belief and value systems have also changed. God's Word has made me more conscious of my thought life. I am being conformed and transformed by renewing my mind, continually giving me a new vantage point of the Messiah and His ways. I don't see Him now as I did in my darkness, as just a man, a religious leader, a teacher. I now have a new perspective and new regard; He is my Lord and Savior. *That new perspective MUST find expression in our lives. As a coach, that expression is known as performance.*

> The renewed man acts upon new principles, by new rules, with new ends, and in a new company. The believer is created anew; his heart is not merely set right, but a new heart is given to him. He is the workmanship of God, created in Christ Jesus unto good works. Though the same as a man, he has changed in his character and conduct. These words must and do mean more than an outward reformation. The man who formerly saw no beauty in the Savior that he should desire him now loves him above all things.[17]
>
> — Matthew Henry

That is the power of perspective. When Father God opens your eyes and allows you to see Christ, you now can experience Him and show Him out.

TIM BROWN

Why Performance Matters

Why am I making such a big deal about adopting a performance perspective? That's an easy answer: Jesus left! Yes, you read that correctly. Okay, look, you don't need to write me any letters; I understand the theology. Jesus now takes up residency in us, and when two or more gather in His name, He is in our presence. Yet the fact remains that Christ, the incarnate, ascended into heaven, leaving us behind to "do His will."

Did you notice that when you accepted Him as Lord and Savior, you remained on the earth? Why? *Performance.* We Christians must act, and the quality of our actions is evident in our performance. Performance is a perspective that needs to be propagated among today's believers as much as ever; the ecosystem depends on it. Del Tackett said, "If we don't really believe and live the truth of God, then our witness will be confusing and misleading."[18]

Maybe you have never thought about it like this before, but God is Spirit. He is invisible. Moreover, the Scripture points out that the unbeliever is blinded. So, how do they hear and see about Christ? Our performance. In the words of Judson Cornwall, "most spiritual decisions are made in solitude with God, but the outworking of those decisions are manifested in public."[19] God has decided to use your life to assist Him in His ultimate plan to restore humankind to Himself.

> The words of Luke, in the first book, O Theophilus,
> I have dealt with all that Jesus began to do and
> teach, until the day when he was taken up, after he
> had given commands through the Holy Spirit to the
> apostles whom he had chosen.
>
> — Acts 1, ESV

Read this quote from the great Finis J. Dake commenting on the scripture above:

> Christ did his works, UNTIL he ascended. AFTER THAT, he continues doing them through Believers by the Holy Spirit baptism they had received.[20]

First, we are created in His image. Second, we were recreated through the new birth and given the Holy Spirit, enabling us to be conformed to His image. Believers performing and behaving the way Christ intended is the objective. Oswald Chambers clarified: "You did not do anything to achieve your salvation, but you must do something to exhibit it."[21]

Oswald's quote had an enormous effect on my perspective. I believe the exhibition of Christ's life and kingdom is our calling. The word "calling"[22] is defined "as a "strong inner impulse toward a particular course," and "exhibit"[23] means "to manifest or display." It is time to apply the scriptures in all departments of life and believe that performing God's Word at an unfathomable level is part of the job description.

> If you have really experienced the Anointed One, and heard his truth, it will be seen in your life; for we know that the ultimate reality[a] is embodied in Jesus.
>
> — Ephesians 4:21, The Passion Translation

I feel so strongly about this addition to your worldview that I genuinely believe you cannot reach your destiny and potential without it. A performance outlook incites us to integrate God's attitudes into our lives so we can become the people of influence we are destined to become. We are talking about divine, life-changing supernatural action. Your calling—your *destiny*—is to become an apex performer of His will and Word in the kingdom of God, bearing fruit that glorifies Jesus.

> My dear brothers and sisters, what good is it if someone claims to have faith but demonstrates no good works to prove it? How could this kind of faith save anyone?
>
> — James 2:14, The Passion Translation

As a mentor, one issue that has always been concerning is that while Christians experience the glorious gift of salvation, only a few will enter His promised land of fulfilled potential. It seems to me that we do not recognize that the pursuit of our potential in Christ should be purposeful in this life. The byproduct of said pursuit is the manifestation and demonstration of His Word and will here on Earth. That is the performance to which I am constantly referring.

Just examine the evidence for a moment. God sent Christ to the cross so that you could be born again and given the Holy Spirit. Did God do all that so you could sit around and wait till it was your turn to go? No. "Salt of the earth,"[24] "the light of the world,"[25] "fishers of men,"[26] "walking worthy,"[27] "bearing much fruit:"[28] all these are Biblical synonyms of apical performance.

Psalm 19:1 (NKJV) says, "The heavens declare his glory," and since you are the apex of His creation, so should you. We have an obligation, as peoples' lives and eternal futures are at stake. "We are His workmanship" as stated in Ephesians 2:10 (NKJV), created for what? "Good works."[29]

As Ephesians 2:10 says, you are God's workmanship. Don't let this important reality slip by. Say it out loud: "I am God's workmanship." Do you know what that means? It means you are the product of God's vision. God has decided what you could be and should be. And through Christ, he has brought about and continues to bring about changes in you in accordance with his picture of what you could and should be. But his vision for you is not complete simply because God has the vision. It has to be made into a reality. So, you have a crucial part in it. [30]

— Andy Stanley

Folks, "His vision made into reality"[31] is High-Performance Christianity.

Why would God "prepare a table for you in the midst of your enemies?"[32] Do you think it would be for us to gloat? Of course, not. He does so to arrest the attention of the unbeliever, to cause them to say, "look what the Lord God has done for them."

God preps the table, but you must participate. You are invited, but you must be willing to take that seat. He has plucked us from destruction. Opening our eyes so that we can pursue our potential, bring Him glory, and make disciples. He did this for His sake and the sake of His kingdom. It has always been about Him, and thank God we get to partake.

"If we cooperate with Him in loving obedience, God will manifest Himself to us, and that manifestation will be the difference between a nominal Christian life and a life radiant with the light of His face. "[33]

A Godly perspective is an impetus that leads to the divine, life-changing supernatural action.

Let your light shine before men in such a way that
they may see your good works and glorify your
Father who is in heaven.

— Matthew 5:16, NASB

"Let your light so shine... – Let your holy life, your pure
conversation, and your faithful instructions be everywhere seen
and known."[34]

That quote sure does sound like a performance to me, need
some more proof?

Always, in all societies, in all business, at home and
abroad, in prosperity and adversity, let it be seen
that you are real Christians. That they may see your
good works – The proper motive to influence is not
simply that we may be seen, but it should be that
our heavenly Father may be glorified.[35]

— Albert Barnes

What Performance Is Not

Before we dive into the different definitions and aspects of the
term performance, I want to clarify this important point: *you are
not saved by your performance.*

I am not advocating performance for approval. As my mentor,
Pastor Mike Millé, would say, "It is the blood of Jesus, plus nothing, that provides access into Heaven. "[36] Salvation is not about
what you did, it is about what HE did. If all you had to do was be
a good person and do good things to go to heaven, there would
have been no need for His suffering on the cross. What I am
encouraging in this book is performing *because of His approval.*

Apex performance is in response to the love of God and the cross. Gary Chapman states it this way, "The third language of gratitude is acts of service—doing something as an expression of gratitude."[37]

> The "laymen" need never think of his humbler
> task as being inferior to that of his minister. Let
> every man abide in the calling wherein he is called,
> and his work will be as sacred as the work of the
> ministry. It is not what a man does that determines
> whether his work is sacred or secular; it is why he
> does it.[38]
>
> — Tozer

Moreover, I am in no way implying that we bring the world's philosophies into the church. However, I do find in some cases that the world borrows successful ideas from the Bible. They may not know it, but it happens all the time. Look at almost every book written about debt, and you will see biblical principles at work.

The problem occurs when Christians don't follow biblical advice. This grave mistake contributes to us underperforming. So, we give back land God told us we could possess. Our job is to filter everything through the Gospel. If it aligns, use it; if it does not, throw it out. Meditation is an excellent example that we will discuss later.

Performance Defined

Here are a few dictionary definitions:

The word modify means "to change in form or character; to alter."[39] Modification is a state of being changed. Dictionary.

com defines performance as "the manner in which or efficiency with which something reacts or fulfills its purpose" and "the manner in which something achieves its intended purpose."[40]

Biblical Definitions of Performance

Now, let's compare the above definitions with that of the Bible. This verse was the gateway scripture for the entire book, and I believe a biblical definition of performance is seen clearly in Paul's letter to the Colossians.

> And so, from the day we heard, we have not ceased to pray for you, asking that you may be filled with the knowledge of his will in all spiritual wisdom and understanding, so as to walk in a manner worthy of the Lord, fully pleasing to him: bearing fruit in every good work and increasing in the knowledge of God; being strengthened with all power, according to his glorious might, for all endurance and patience with joy; giving thanks[a] to the Father, who has qualified you[b] to share in the inheritance of the saints in light. He has delivered us from the domain of darkness and transferred us to the Kingdom of his beloved Son.
>
> — Colossians 1:9-13, ESV

Please pay attention to the term "so as to." The phrase means to perform some type of action.[41] For example, I treat my wife with love and kindness "so as to" sleep in the same bed.

My specific objective with this book is for us to make the connection between knowledge and behavior. The idea of spiritual wisdom is to affect how we walk. The lack of connection is the root as to why we rarely reach potential. *Our salvation should produce materialization!*

An accurate biblical perspective is to realize that He wants us to perform His pleasure. Best-selling author Bruce Wilkerson, who wrote *Secrets of the Vine*, states the following: *"For years, I read John 15:1-2 as a general call to Christians to bring others to Christ. But there's no reason to restrict Jesus's meaning of fruit to winning souls. I have traced the words fruit and good works in the Bible, and they're used interchangeably."[2]*

Enhancing performance in His chosen field for us creates an enlarged opportunity to extend the kingdom. We gain the ability to influence people for Him, allowing the church to regain the ground it has handed over to the world.

Targeted for High Performance

[16] You did not choose me, but I chose you and appointed you that you should go and bear fruit and that your fruit should abide, so that whatever you ask the Father in my name, he may give it to you.

—John 15:16, ESV

We were targeted before the foundation of the world to become an Apex Performer. He has assigned an ecosystem for which we are responsible. God has "apprehended" us for a relationship to fulfill His plans for us, for He has a specific objective. The plans are part of the reason He saved us and are vital to the ecosystem. Do you think God would allow your eyes to be opened to spend eternity in heaven but be insignificant here on earth? I don't think so. That would be a corrupted perspective. His desire is for us to be the "light"[43] set on high. Time to turn up the dimmer switch. Don't overthink it; agree with it.

High Performance Is an Obligation

I believe we are obligated to pursue our potential in Christ Jesus. You may be thinking the word "obligated" is a little harsh, but remember, the mission is to glorify Him. Our lives are not our own. We gave up the right to ourselves, allowing the Spirit to lead our actions and thought life; we have been purchased by blood. Judson Cornwall, in his book *Worship As David Lived It*, stated that "God has accepted the responsibility to move the heart of man with his word, but it's man's responsibility to respond obediently to that work."[44] We sing songs like "Jesus Paid it All." Christ did indeed pay it all for us; shouldn't we live like He did?

The Big Picture

"Through sin, man was driven out of Eden, away from the presence and fellowship of God. God in His mercy sought from the beginning to restore the broken fellowship."[45]

— Andrew Murray

As touched on earlier, I was taught by my mentors that God has a strategic plan to win back His enemies unto Himself. As you can probably tell, I've taken that teaching to heart. I believe it is God's mission for us.

That priority was demonstrated to us by God determining the crucifixion of His only Son. The entire biblical message is prevalent with God's desire to commune, transform, and reconcile others to the King.

Therefore, we are to live a Spirit-guided life, filled with unimaginable outcomes, whereby you create success and influence for His glory. He gave us 750 precious promises; let's go ahead and realize them.

Worship is expressed by our lifestyle. The meaning of true worship is not singing songs. That may be an avenue, but true worship is being good at whatever God has you to do. Christians must discipline themselves to become hearers and doers. God wants to perform incredible things with us and for us, and the beauty of it is that anyone who is a believer can be used. We all can reach our potential and accomplish what he has for us. God does not discriminate.

CHAPTER 3

The Third Imperative: The Progress

For everyone who listens with an open heart will receive progressively more revelation until he has more than enough. But those who don't listen with an open, teachable heart, even the understanding that they think they have will be taken from them.

— Matthew 13:12, TPT

Potential Is Prescribed

Performance and potential are prescribed to us as a commandment by Jesus Himself. Like all good Chief Executive Officers, He gave us a mission statement: not stay or sit, but to "go," and going requires motion. Not the circular movement that involves wandering in this world's wilderness for years, then retirement. Instead, He commissions genuine, spirit-led action, following an appointed path. "Go and make disciples,"[46] performers, doers of His will, not just church attenders.

As we determine to renew our minds, our actions become more associated with His will. By performing His Word, we begin to experience its beautiful byproducts and benefits. Christians who commit to the discipleship process start to transition from a system of darkness to a system of light. Non-believers look upon the progress, causing them to consider Christ for salvation. Faith is to be dynamically displayed for the world to see, or at the very least, the ecosystem in which God has placed us.

We as believers must get back to actively demonstrating faith as we deliberately practice our craft to expand and enlarge. Purposeful abiding in the presence of God will result in our world-view being evident and arrayed.

Advancing the kingdom is accomplished by learning and obeying His voice and Word, especially when it does not make sense. Believing in God and performing the Word, especially against natural reasons, allows an opportunity for the supernatural to flourish.

Increase

But continue to grow and increase in God's grace and intimacy with our Lord and Savior, Jesus Christ. [a] May he receive all the glory both now and until the day eternity begins.

— 2 Peter 3:18, TPT

We see the same message throughout this entire Scripture: "continue to grow and increase." These words are not suggestions; instead, they are orders from headquarters. Given to us out of love, yes, but they are orders. We are to move from faith to faith, level to level, ever keeping the goal of being conformed to His image at the forefront.

"Apex Predators have few, if any, predators themselves, and typically not once they are fully grown."[47]

— Colin Dunn

Apex performers practice progressive faith by recognizing this important pattern of moving away from old life and self-consciousness to new life and God-consciousness, which is the epitome of spiritual maturity. As He increases and we decrease, we become unstoppable.

Progression on Display

The epistles to the Church in Thessalonica are often referred to by people primarily concerning end times, and rightly so, as the book plays a prominent role regarding eschatology. However, that is only a part of the story behind this body of believers. These people were high performers. The Church in Thessalonica was known as a model church.

In this letter, the Church petitioners were lauded by Paul. Why were they held in such high esteem? Because they not only listened to Paul's words, but they *executed his teachings*. They certainly were not a church full of perfect Christians, but it is obvious they were progressing ones.

Here is a bit of Matthew Henry's commentary:

> … for what he esteemed them and thanked God;
> namely, the increase of their faith, and love, and
> patience. In his former epistle, he gave thanks
> for their faith, love, and patience; here, he gives
> thanks for the increase of all those graces; that is
> why they're not only true Christians but growing
> Christians. Note, where there is the truth of grace,
> there will be an increase in it. The Path of the just
> is as the shining light, which shines more and more
> unto the perfect day. And where there is an increase
> of the grace, God must have all the glory of it. We
> are as much indebted to him for the improvement

of grace and the progress of that good work as we are for the first work of grace and the very beginning of it.[48]

I love this language — *"Not only were they true but growing, where there is grace, there is increase."* What a word, and what a description, hopefully, to be said of us someday.

The Dake Bible, a bestselling classic study Bible, and commentary states it this way in a summary of 1st Thessalonians: *"converts were mainly gentiles who became outstanding examples of demonstrating God's power taught by Paul to all believers."*[49]

Pondering Progression

My dear brothers and sisters, what good is it if someone claims to have faith but demonstrates no good works to prove it? How could this kind of faith save anyone?

— James 2:14, The Passion Translation

It is one thing to discuss how the scriptures support biblical performance and how the Word endorses a performance perspective to be added to our Christian life. However, it is something else to demonstrate this fruit in ourselves and those who reside in our ecosystem. So, the question becomes, "How do we progress?" How do we advance from believer to disciple, move from captive to deliverer, and influence our assigned area?

Learn from the Master

One option is to look at a favorite subject of mine, known as collision dynamics. Don't worry; I am not going to give you a golf lesson. In fact, you don't need to know anything about golf to understand the significance of what I am about to share. You see, I believe the above picture of the golf ball and club represents a catalyst to a miraculous life for all of us. So, what exactly can we glean?

All throughout the New Testament, Jesus would consistently take the natural items of the era and use them to unpack the supernatural. This is arguably His preferred method of sharing revelation in the gospels. I am simply modeling the King's favorite teaching technique by extracting the manna embedded in the image. This next piece of Scripture captures His technique effectively.

> For sure, I tell you, unless a seed falls into the ground and dies, it will only be a seed. If it dies, it will give much grain.
>
> —John 12:24, NLT

We know that in this verse, Jesus is using an agricultural example of a seed, crushed by ground pressure, as symbolism to share the supernatural. He is talking about His death, burial, and resurrection, as well as the life that will sprout from it.

The items of our time and age may differ, but the principles and revelation pass through time and are still powerfully operating today. The Bible is NOT outdated; the vehicles of revelation have changed. Since golf is my type of "agriculture," I want to copy Christ.

Because I am particularly passionate about golf, I will use the subject of *collision dynamics* to make my point. So, how can the collision occurring in this photograph assist us in becoming apex performers?

What if I told you the club represents my golf instrument, and the Bible represents my God instrument? Now, what if I said both instruments were constructed, designed, and created for the same purpose: *impact*? Get it?

In the natural realm, it merely looks like a picture of the golf club encountering a golf ball. However, in the supernatural, there is so much more.

The image of the impact interval is symbolic of a Kingdom Collision. Kingdom Collisions are instances whereby God's

Word comes in direct contact with our human nature. *What is represented in this picture is God's Word dealing a devastating blow to an anti-kingdom belief system, a belief system composed of human tradition, reason, and demonic strategies. His Word is violently and swiftly crashing into our own round object that sits between our ears, our minds.* Its chief target is our carnal nature. After all, you cannot be like Jesus unless you start thinking like Jesus.

Properly Apply

Here is the catch, any teacher worth his salt knows that to create a powerful, efficient, and enduring impact, one must properly apply the instrument. The same is true with Scripture, and I call this artful administration of the Bible "skillful wielding."

> ...if the ax is dull and its edge unsharpened, more strength is needed, but SKILL will bring success.
>
> — Ecclesiastes 10:10, NIV

Skillful wielding is not just the accumulation of daily bread but the ability to recognize, apply, and obey. Artfully handling the instrument is directly proportional to our ability to experience a meaningful and glorifying life. As a matter of fact, it was Derek Prince who stated, *"it is the response of the believer that will determine the effect of God's word."* [52] I don't care if you're a carpenter, a pastor, or a painter; it's how you skillfully wield the instrument that will enable you to "walk in a manner worthy." [53]

Kingdom Physics

I am going to get a little technical in the following few paragraphs to detail how this works. My hope is to break down these encounters in such a way you will have increased awareness and respond accordingly. After all, it is easier to perform a task if we understand the backdrop. As we pull back the curtain even more and peer into the dynamics of the collision, I trust you will start to see invaluable phases and applications. If I am successful, this image will go a long way to helping you become a "skillful wielder."

Initial Contact

[18] Remember not the former things, nor consider the things of old. [19] Behold, I am doing a new thing; now it springs forth, do you not perceive it?

— Isaiah 43:18-19, ESV

The first is called the "initial contact" phase (see picture 51). In this phase, the instrument (Word) comes into first contact with the intended object, which is usually our comfort zone. God is very often looking to do the "new thing" in and among us, but the primary step is to *perceive it is happening*.

In my view, these collisions are numerous, occurring daily. They provide us with divine opportunities to practice and eventually manifest the supernatural in our ecosystem. For example, have you ever had a thought run through your mind to pray for a stranger at Walmart or some other public venue? That was most likely an opportunity to step out, and react to the divine prod. How did that make you feel? Was there an awkward hesitancy? Did you respond to the prompt? Did you try to reason with God? What happens when God wants you to give some type of possession or money? Was that just a thought?

Obviously, the supernatural is not natural, and it will usually make our "flesh" a bit uncomfortable. Remember when Saul tried to put his armor on David? David remarked it was "foreign" to him. Why? I would argue that David was uncomfortable fighting like everyone else. His uneasiness existed because he was so intimate with God; his familiarity created freedom that the common thinking, armor, and battle tactics could not provide. We should strive to get to that level. A level where we recognize the natural is uncomfortable for us.

Tithing is a perfect example of a kingdom collision. How so? Most people fear *"running out of money before running out of the month,"* so they succumb to the feeling induced by the worry and do not respond to the command. The result is the same fear and lack.

I can recall times being at my house and watching television when a thought goes through my mind to turn it off and pray. I can tell you that the idea did not come from me. The "me" in "me" just wanted to chill. After a long day at work, the last thing I wanted to do was pray while my favorite show was airing. Parenting, relationships, finances, and health are opportunities to apply the Scripture. God gives us lots of chances, which we need to perceive.

Skill

On a deeper level, wielding can save your life. A few years ago, I almost lost my life. I was very close to drowning. My wife and children were watching from the beach. It was a very close call, and I did not think I was going to make it.

There are times when the thought of them watching me die creeps into my mind, and it really disturbs me. I get this terrible feeling inside. However, due to my faith and foundation in the word, I immediately turn my mind back to God, for He is perfect peace. I perceive that everything in my life is "Father filtered." When the thoughts of "what if" come upon me, I immediately know I am in a collision, and I have a choice to respond appropriately by setting my mind on Him. I also have the power because of the Holy Spirit. Since "greater is He that is in me than he that is in the world"[54] and "anything born of God overcomes the world."[55] I do not have to continue in that painful state. I have authority, power, and the ability to cancel that line of thinking. As you will learn later in greater detail, my spirit man is in charge and tells my soul what to think. What the enemy meant for evil; God will turn it for good.

I can go on and on with many more examples, but my real objective is for you to see that collisions occur frequently, and we just need to pay closer attention.

As we get back to impact, the first step is knowing we are involved in a collision. As mentioned in the earlier examples, we should take notice of the sensation we have in response to the Word. I'm not suggesting we rely on feelings. I am simply stating that we should pay attention to those thoughts and feelings associated with the command of Christ. This is the practical application of "taking every thought captive."[56] Typically, the unnaturalness of the supernatural world can be a signal that a collision is imminent.

Transformation Phase

*"Be not conformed but transformed
by the renewing of your mind."* [57]

The second phase is the all-important transformation phase. In this phase, the morphed sphere in the previous image represents our thought life, and as you can see from the picture, our carnal nature has been struck by a violent blow. There is nothing more dynamic than God's Word impacting a worldview, a philosophy, and a perspective. It is a game-changer. Why? Pre-existing worldviews are literally experiencing a dramatic state change. Look at the deformity of the golf ball. *God's instrument is assaulting the original condition, and a massive conversion ensues.*

Transference Phase

The third phase is the *"transference phase."* Now that we are aware of the collisions and find ourselves knee-deep, a transference anointing is released. By the way, this is my favorite phase, and it is invaluable for reaching Godly potential. It's not complicated; it's simple physics, kingdom physics.

I once heard Golf Professional Mike Hebron sum up God's Laws of Motion (discovered by Sir Isaac Newton) in this way:

"If you create a force and can control the direction of that force, you can control the direction of what that force hits." [58]

Examples? Think about an expert pool player. When the skilled player moves the stick, a force is created. As they control the direction of that stick, control is gained over the cue ball. The result is the pocketing of the balls. The same goes for an elite golfer. The elite player swings the club with precision, creating a force. By controlling the direction of that force, one can impart instructions to the golf ball affecting its direction, trajectory, and velocity.

God's Word is no different!

When a Christian wields the instrument, they create a force. The more precise the applied force, the more influence they have. Kingdom momentum is created as we direct the Word to our circumstance, situation, and area of influence. Executing the movement properly creates an environment that asserts Godly pressure. That pressure is why transformation and transference occur. That pressure is why we walk through the church doors; God's love is putting conviction on our hearts as He is drawing us to Him.

Please take note that, in image 51, the instrument is in contact with the sphere. As a result of this *direct and intimate contact,* a transference is produced. During this transfer phase, an impartation of instruction from one body to the other is initiated. Exchange is taking place, and supernatural instructions are transferred from the instrument to us!

The God instrument transmits an updated set of coordinates, kingdom coordinates. Every time you seek His face, every time you obey the Word, every time you respond to the prompt of the Holy Ghost, every time you pray for your kids, every time you identify with Him when you are persecuted, every time you ask Him to rebuke the devourer, every time you renew your mind, every time you praise and worship, every time you move by faith and not by sight, you create a force or a dynamic that will directly influence the object you intend to impact. The impact starts with us and then the world; it is transference.

As we transition toward his image and motives, the more influence we transfer to the community. That was a considerable point of Pentecost: to be filled with His power, be transformed, and turn the world upside down.

The Launch Phase

In summary, we first perceive a collision, and then we apply God's Word skillfully, regardless of feelings. The correct application of which imparts divine wisdom, and then we get our final phase. I call this final phase the "Launch phase."

We can see, in the last picture, the object that's being transformed is now regaining its shape and being *renewed* as it is launched out. Notice how the object of the collision is sent totally *restored*.

The renewed mind is set out, on a new path, on a new trajectory with incredible power, armed with an apostolic objective and a mission to make disciples and glorify God. Revelation is now guiding the renewed mind; therefore, there are no limitations on how high one can fly, how fast one can get there, and what direction to go in. It's called kingdom physics, and that is how the Bible works.

Mastery

Progress still requires a level of mastery at applying and obeying God's Word. I mentioned mastery earlier, but let's take a closer look. The word mastery indicates "total command"[60] of the subject and/or instrument. The word *wield* means "to employ with authority."[61] Therefore, to accomplish our purpose as image-bearers, we need to continue developing a formidable skill set composed of revelation, prayer, and a worldview based on truth. To perform our potential, the Word needs to be deftly employed. A mind focused on enhancing technique, acquiring skill, practice, and most importantly, revelation is the recipe for kingdom success.

Ezra - A Skillful Wielder

Ezra 7:6 (NKJV) says, "this Ezra came up from Babylon; and he was a SKILLED scribe in the Law of Moses, which the Lord God of Israel had given. The King granted him all his requests, according to the hand of the Lord his God upon him."

Take the biblical example of the person Ezra. Talk about one of the premier wielders in the canon. I could choose from a plethora of powerful apex performers in the Bible, but one of my favorites is Ezra.

Ezra was a "skilled scribe," [62] and Ezra chapter seven must be one of the great chapters in Scripture. Why? Few people realize the importance of a scribe's occupation. After all, by the time Jesus was on the scene in the New Testament, their reputation was tarnished.

The fact is that the job of the scribe was critical. Scribes were charged with carefully studying and dictating God's covenants. The occupation was to meticulously copy the text and the manuscripts, passing it down from generation to generation. The copies had to be accurate, and exact.

Furthermore, Ezra is credited with authoring multiple books of the Bible and is regarded as a major part of the "Great Assembly," a group said to be responsible for organizing the Hebrew canon. Make no mistake about it, scribes were anointed contributors to the Bible today, and Ezra was one of the best.

I trust you can detect some insight into Ezra's high-performance life. However, what caught my attention in the book of Ezra is how the Holy Spirit seems to repeat this similar message: "The wisdom in your hand."[63] If you read the entirety of chapter seven, you will see where twice the same verbiage is used. This is important because whenever God repeats, He is trying to get our attention for sure.

Hand-Eye Coordination the Key to Discipleship

I think it is obvious that the "wisdom that is in your hand" is symbolic of the Word.

Therefore, if we're not experiencing mastery in our relationships, health, finances, and most importantly, intimacy with God, you can bet somewhere along the way there's been an improper utilization of the instrument.

As a motor skill coach, I would suggest that the issue is not one of faith but rather one of coordination—specifically, an eye-hand issue. Eye-hand? Yes. Hang in there for a second; I know what you're thinking; *what in the heck does that have to do with spiritual growth?* EVERYTHING! Read the definition:

> The ability of the vision system to coordinate the information received through the eyes to control, guide, and direct the hands in the accomplishment of a given task, such as handwriting or catching a ball.[64]

In the physical realm, our eyes respond to visual input, gathering information and coordinating with muscles to create the movement of your hand. That is true, but, in the Kingdom realm, the relationship between the two is deeper; one affects the other. So let me give you the supernatural version.

When I became a Christian, I knew nothing about the Bible. After all, Biblical knowledge is not a prerequisite for salvation. God, in His incredible mercy, rushed in and opened the eyes of my understanding.[65] Instantly, I became a new creation. But like all newborns, my eye-hand skills needed time for development.

Lacking coordination is why we grasp, stumble, and move with trepidation in our youth. Devoid of a discipleship mentality, our fearless and joyful walk can get a little shaky and unstable. Therefore, to balance our precious faith with a life that emanates Christ, we must learn how *to coordinate our new sight with the instrument that is in hand.*

In God's world, there is an interplay between what you see (perspective) and what is in your hand (the Bible). Our spiritual eyes receive invaluable revelation from the Word in our hand, enabling us to achieve new movements toward becoming like Christ. Since we gravitate towards our focus, "let thine eye be single[66]" taking in revelation from the words of Jesus. Now we may look at life with Christ-like clarity, empowering us to function as originally intended, in lockstep with the King. As God's people, we should follow Ezra's lead, pursuing mastery with His Word, the precision instrument in our hands.

Uncoordinated

> While most people own a Bible and know some of its content, our research found that most Americans have little idea how to integrate core biblical principles to form a unified and meaningful response to the challenges and opportunities of life.[67]
>
> — George Barna

Our ability to coordinate and develop our hand-eye is significant in showing Christ to the world. As a coach, I often look at data, and the studies reveal we have some issues. There exists some distressing information that shows many of us are underperforming. It seems we are struggling a bit with our coordination. For example, according to George Barna and his research team, studies show that:

- less than twenty-five percent of born-again Christians use the Bible for decision making[68]
- only one of every seven believes in using the Bible as their moral compass, and that moral truth is absolute[69]
- ninety-one percent of all born-again adults do not have a biblical worldview[70]
- ninety-eight percent of all born-again teenagers do not have a biblical worldview.[71]

The stats are disturbing. As a coach, I want to help others be more organized.

Position versus Alignment

In wrapping up this chapter, I want to share one final thought. Homer Kelley, a prominent golf pedagogue, introduced the concepts of position-based golf and alignment-based golf and said that "alignment golf simply smothers position golf."[72] I believe the same is true with Christianity, and this concept is a significant component to improving our coordination in Christ. I call it "position versus alignment." Let me explain.

Several years ago, God impressed upon me that in my life, I was making a similar mistake that many of us PGA professionals used to make in teaching the golf swing.

What was that mistake? For the longest time, we were teaching the swing based mainly on a positional model. The emphasis was placed on getting folks in the correct positions during the swing. Was this bad? No, but there is a weakness in that philosophy, a weakness that Kelley so eloquently pointed out. *As it relates to the golf swing, position alone won't get you the outcome you seek. Only proper alignment with the instrument will yield the desired result.*

Why is that a big deal? God showed me that alignment was missing from my worldview. Over the years, I have seen the phenomenon present in the Church. Christians can parallel golfers: *We can be in all the correct positions and still be out of alignment.*

Directing attention SOLELY on the positional aspects of salvation *without* also prioritizing potential, development, and discipleship will too often result in lower-level performance, like that mentioned in the Barna data.

Don't get me wrong, I am utterly grateful for my position in Christ, but salvation is the beginning of my new life. Although the most important of God's gifts, once born anew, we must include alignment as part of our perspective and turn our attention to accurately aligning with God, DOING what he teaches.

To prove my theory, here is a glance at our current position in Christ:

- "Greater is He"[73]
- "Same Spirit that raised Jesus from the Dead"[74]
- "Saved by grace"[75]
- "Access to the mind of Christ"[76]
- "Anointing to know all things"[77]
- "Plans to prosper"[78]
- "Creative speech"[79]

Looking at the characteristics above, I ask you; could we be in a better position to reach our potential? I do not think so. Yes, at one time, we were sinners saved by grace, but now, we are the "carriages that carry the King."

My take is that due to the gift of salvation accomplished on the cross and the belief in the work Christ performed, we are automatically translated, positionally, as a new creation. Therefore, our position cannot be the problem in our lack of maturity. Moreover, we have the deposit of faith, so faith cannot be the culprit.

The fact is, regardless of our situation or feelings right now, if, in Christ, we are in the best position possible. God's deliverer exists inside us, His name is the Holy Spirit, and through Him, all things are possible.

What keeps us from reaching our potential and performing at Christ-like levels has more to do with our willingness and awareness of aligning with Christ and his word. Christ qualifies us positionally, so we could have the same capacity to carry out the good works.

Please hear me; I'm not attempting to be insensitive. I get how your circumstances could be challenging as you read this book. A loss of a loved one, an evil report, financial hardship, maybe you're going through a divorce. I know, all too well, that this life can be full of difficulties, trials, and tribulations. However, that doesn't change your standing or positioning in Christ. The Holy Spirit is more powerful than our physical circumstances. The key is to align ourselves with what He says, especially regarding what He says about us, and to exchange our worldview and EXECUTE. The map to spiritual maturity must include moving from position to alignment.

CHAPTER 4

The Fourth Imperative: The Paradigm

Now may the God of peace Himself sanctify[a] you completely; and may your whole spirit, soul, and body be preserved blameless at the coming of our Lord Jesus Christ.

— 1 Thessalonians 5:23, NKJV

We can now turn our attention to the following imperative of potential: understanding our true design.

The Fable (How This Book Came About)

In the beginning, as a new Christian chasing God and spending time trying to become a good husband, father, and top teaching professional, I wanted to be a good provider. I was blessed doing what I loved. I was very successful, coaching, winning multiple PGA awards, and ranked among the best.

Since most of my adult life is dedicated to seeing my students improve and progress, I was eager to expand my knowledge base; I traveled near and far, learning as much as possible about the swing. After all, being a good coach is hard work, and you must be knowledgeable in several different subjects. For example, teachers must understand the basic functional movement of the body to prescribe correct motor patterns that the person can physically achieve. We need to have a working knowledge of physics and geometry to understand the mechanics of the swing and the golf ball's flight. We need to know how people learn and then simulate the training. It took years to build this inventory. However, the more I taught, the more I became aware that enhancing the performance of my clients was much more than just getting people to hit the ball better. I had to get them to perform.

Paralleling this trajectory of becoming a top teacher, I was heavily involved in my faith and attending a remarkable Church—a Church where Pastor Michael Millé held advanced degrees in psychology. The same Church hosted a "School of Ministry" right on site. Therein, my wife and I enrolled in several courses. I had become certified in a few different areas of the psychological genre.

Again, I was blessed to be associated with the incredibly gifted and anointed people who gave me keen insight into the Scripture, aiding my walk as a Christian. Then one day, something happened. I refer to it as my burning bush.

In 2011, I was sitting in my living room, watching Jason Duffner vie for the PGA near Atlanta. I was pulling for him because he worked with Chuck Cook, a friend, and a master teacher from Texas. Jason was playing great on one of the most challenging courses in the country. With four holes left in the event, things changed. Jason, who had been in total control of his game and leading the field, proceeded to falter on the last few holes, thereby losing the championship. It was difficult to watch; my heart went out for both Jason and Chuck.

As a teacher, I was fascinated as to what triggered the demise. I started to run through the years of golf swing hacks cataloged in my brain. I was intrigued; it just did not make sense to me that Jason suddenly lost his swing. I could only imagine the pressure of that moment and what was happening to him. His life was about to change forever. I wondered if Jason was looking ahead. Did he start to realize he was going to win? Something went amiss, and it manifested itself at a critical juncture? I remember turning to my wife, sitting on the couch next to me, and saying to her, "Kim, I have to revamp my teaching. I must look at everything I've been doing. What happened was not a swing change; it was a change of state."

The event stuck with me. I continued to ponder what I had seen, but things were different for me from that point on. A new awareness had been born inside me; I started to pay attention to elements beyond just the mechanics of motor skills.

The Fire

Around that time, Peter Hanson was leading the Masters, sleeping on the lead on the eve of the finals. After the Saturday round, the media interviewed him; that interview, coupled with what happened to Jason Duffner, absolutely changed things for me. Hanson had uttered the common phrase, the words I had heard a million times before by top performers in every arena. The words he spoke rang loudly in my ears. It is a phrase often repeated in sports *"I just need to control my emotions, I am playing very well, but I need to control my emotions."*

So frequently, I hear the world's best repeating those lines. At the elite levels of sports, that phrase is constant prose. Almost every major event elicited the same response as Hanson's. The emphasis was not the swing or technique but controlling one's emotions. It was this emphasis that had triggered a new pursuit in my life. I now recognized that my two great passions, God's Word, and coaching, were now going to collide.

I believe God impressed upon me that I possessed life-changing spiritual truths due to my relationship with Him, my reading of His Word, and the tremendous people who had influenced me. I knew that through Christ, I could contribute to myself, my ecosystem, and the body, regarding authentic emotional control.

Why? Because *Christians have a serious advantage in controlling emotions, and it begins with our true design.*

The Flaw

> He was in the world, and the world was made
> through him, the world did not recognize him.
>
> — 1 John 1:10, NIV

As I continued to embark on this journey, it did not take me very long to realize severe defects in orthodox emotional management philosophy. Two problems stood out right away.

First, Jesus and the Bible simply play no serious role in the battle for the mind and emotional management. I understand why much of the world doesn't accept Christ, and I am conscious of the spiritual underpinnings. I get it; people don't believe what we believe. I am also aware that the "god of this age has blinded many eyes.[80]" But seriously, just think about this for a second. The most influential person in the history of the world, the inventor of faith, is essentially being removed from this field.

Jim Rohn, the father of personal development coaching, often says, *"success leaves clues."* In an area where topics like faith, trust, belief, commitment, acceptance, imagery, focus, and vision are prominent, Christ is diminished to an "outside agency."[81] He is not part of the match; there is no "following of the clues," that is for sure.

Secondly, since so many psychologists, sports psychologists, performance coaches, counselors, and educators are closed to Christ's teachings, *their perspective of the human blueprint is incomplete and inherently flawed, rendering the analyses less potent.*

The popular, worldly approach to regulating emotional control is assigned to the mind. Primarily focusing on "mental toughness." Phrases like "get out of your mind" or "train your brain" all prioritize the use of the mind; that message is insufficient. Without acknowledgment of a spiritual realm, there can be no actual freeing of the mind, will, or emotions that run our lives. Mental strategies alone are lacking and do not always align with God's Word. So, what are the so-called experts missing?

The answer is that without the Holy Spirit, they can only regard us as *dual entities*. A dual entity? Yes, a body and soul, which is a false conclusion. According to the Scripture, the truth is that believers are triune beings, not dual entities, complete with body, soul, and spirit.

The Failure

Beware lest anyone cheat you through philosophy and empty deceit, according to the tradition of men, according to the basic principles of the world, and not according to Christ.

— Colossians 2:8, NKJV

The failure not to consider what is happening in the spiritual dimension can only lead to natural outcomes. Hence, I am concerned that Christians are partaking in the same failed and fragmented advice followed by the world. According to Oswald Chambers, "Much of the misery in our Christian life comes not because the devil tackles us, but because we have never understood the simple laws of our make-up."[82]

Chasing incomplete information can incite us to run to the darkness, looking for the light. As a result, we have segregated our faith, which is devastating to our potential. Compartmentalization is the kryptonite to Christianity. Yes, we do have a form of kryptonite.

Thus, you nullify the word of God by your tradition that you have handed down. And you do many things like that.

— Mark 7:13, NIV

Continuing in the "traditional" ways of thinking separates Church from the state, and in this case, I am referring to our mental and emotional state. That type of estrangement will bring havoc to your life and impotence to your witness. Thinking the Bible only applies to religious formalities, we fall for the myth that it has no place in our day-to-day life. We are buying the lie that it is outdated dogma not applicable in every situation.

God's Cause

God has enlisted us to champion His cause. We are enrolled in the mission of bringing heaven to earth. That is the race we are running. We all possess free will and a choice to move from spectator to participant. We can choose not to engage, but we will watch the ecosystem shrivel up and die around us. Remember, lives are at stake. How about that for pressure?

So, whether you are a Christian athlete, lawyer, plumber, CEO, stay-at-home dad, businesswoman, male or female, adult, or adolescent, becoming more acquainted with our true triune design and design functions is the recipe for true emotional control. Oswald Chambers stated that "In spiritual issues, it is customary for us to put God first, but we tend to think that it is inappropriate and unnecessary to put Him first in the practical, everyday issues of our lives."[83]

Demonstrating the fruit of the Spirit is part of the plan, no matter the occupation or situation.

Some people think their vision has no such spiritual significance. For example, somebody might say, "I'm not hoping to start a church or ministry or anything like that. I'm trying to get a business off the ground. What does that have to do with 'God's overarching vision for the world'?" From God's perspective, there are no spiritual versus nonspiritual components of your life. He makes no distinction. There is no secular division of your life. You are a spiritual being. Therefore, everything you are involved in has spiritual overtones. He sees you holistically.[84]

— Andy Stanley

Pay attention to phrases such as "He makes no distinction" and "He sees us holistically." Pastor Stanley is correct that it is not God who makes such divisions.

We need to *unsubscribe* from the ungodly ideology that we are only body and soul composed. Saying things like "God has better things to do" or "He doesn't care about my game" or "my job" is counter-productive and double-minded. He cares! He cares about you, your character, motives, and conduct, and He cares about those people you are supposed to reach. We need to see the bigger picture so we can manifest the King's vision.

The secret of a Christian's life is that the
supernatural becomes natural in Him as a result
of the grace of God, and the experience of this
becomes evident in the practical, everyday details of
life, not in times of intimate fellowship with God.
And when we come in contact with things that
create confusion and a flurry of activity, we find to
our own amazement that we have the power to stay
wonderfully poised even in the center of it all.[85]

—Oswald Chambers

The Fall—How Did We Get Here?

Genesis 2:17 (NLT) says, "… except the tree of the knowledge of good and evil. If you eat its fruit, you are sure to die."

I mentioned earlier that our first parents did not die when they ate the forbidden fruit. On the contrary, they went on to live very long lives. So, is God a liar? Of course, not. Due to the fall, the spirit/inner man went completely dormant and died. Consequently, the pandemic of independence was passed down from generation to generation. Emanating from this iniquity were devastating consequences and the cause of every issue facing humanity today.

The Fallout

It wasn't that long ago that you lived in the religion,
customs, and values of this world, obeying the dark
ruler of the earthly realm who fills the atmosphere
with his authority and works diligently in the
hearts of those who are disobedient to the truth

of God. The corruption that was in us from birth
was expressed through the deeds and desires of our
self-life. We lived by whatever natural cravings and
thoughts our minds dictated, living as rebellious
children subject to God's wrath like everyone else.

— Ephesians 2:2-3, The Passion Translation

Due to our disobedience, the corresponding union of our trinity was severed, causing mankind to be led by our soul and body. Open access to God is now blocked. Meaning that from this one moment, unless regenerated through faith in Christ, humans are now directed, guided, and ruled by tainted minds and emotions. Segregated from the Spirit by sin, our operating system, now fragmented, has opened the door wide to be hacked with a code riddled in self-preservation and self-focus. We then became self-governing and independent. Seduce and separate was Satan's strategy all along.

Reaching our potential is impossible because we have wallowed in a soulish-based system, a self-craving body, and a self-centered soul. The path of ungodly habits, life strategies, patterns, thoughts, beliefs, values, and customs "seems right" but ends in tragedy.

[2] Do not conform to the pattern of this world, but
be transformed by the renewing of your mind. Then
you will be able to test and approve what God's will
is—his good, pleasing and perfect will.

— Romans 12:2, New International Version (NIV)

We were never designed to conform. The world's pattern is founded on the sand of humanism and self-reliance. This tactic leads to frustration and caps potential because we were never oriented to be unallied.

The Functionality

Unfortunately, my experience as a Sunday school and small group leader for more than twenty years is that very few Christians are aware of the biblical tripartite teaching and how it works.

> The distinction between these three elements of our personality is little understood by MOST Christians. The Bible provides us with a unique kind of "mirror," which reveals their nature and interrelationship and shows us how each is intended to function. Failure to use this mirror correctly exposes us to much inner frustration and disharmony.[86]
>
> — Derek Prince

Getting a firm hold on the functionality of our design will spark an entirely new spiritual effectiveness in our lives. Once fully engaged in this paradigm shift of perspective, we will discover absolute authority over the soul and the body, for we possess the capacity to separate soul and Spirit accurately. This concept is obviously missing in the world's philosophy and approach towards managing emotions, giving Christians real power to witness.

This regenerated spirit located at the center of man's being is what we call the inward man. Secondly, outside the sphere of this inward man indwelt by God is the soul. Its functions are thoughts, emotions, and will. Thirdly, the outermost man is our physical body characterized by its external insight, instincts of sight, sound, smell, taste, and touch.[87]

— Watchman Nee

Don't just read this next part and not add it to your life. As a triune being, God does not, nor should we, *regard the brain and mind as the primary "signal-caller."* The brain does not have the authority assigned to it by psychologists, counselors, educators.

"It will also help to realize that God in designing man originally, intended for a man's spirit to be his home or dwelling place. So, the Holy Spirit, by making his union with the human spirit was to govern the soul. Then further, the spirit through the soul would use the body as a means expressing God's life and purpose.[88]

Many Christians are not aware of this fact. The key is to recognize the chain of command: the Spirit should oversee the soul, and the soul should oversee the body. That's a superior advantage we have as Christ-followers. Notice I said Christ-followers, implying the spiritual order of things. We follow Him.

In the original pattern of creation, there was a descending relationship. God moved upon man's spirit; his spirit moved upon his soul; his soul directed his body.[89]

— Derek Prince

Generally, the body is constantly receiving information through the five senses. Those senses are communicating with the soul. Before Christ, that would be the extent of it. The "old nature" would do what seems right, feels right, etc. However, as believers, we are equipped with a divine "*inner man.*" As an awakened spirit, we can be confident in the pure governance of the divine nature housed within.

Christian, you are complete. Therefore, align yourself with what He suffered so much to say. This completeness allows us to decipher any situation and apply the Word accordingly. The key is to recognize the heavenly hierarchy given to us by the King Himself, following the chain. Each of these offices has a unique role to play and a specific function to perform. Knowing how each part works allows us to discern and obey His will enabling us to accomplish and establish the kingdom here on earth.

Don't forget; there is order to everything. God made you with a purpose in mind. God formed you to be Triune so you could relate to Him and then function accordingly. Bypassing the Spirit will not allow you to exhibit the supernatural because the "seed produces after its own kind. "[90] If you are going to function as a spiritual being, you must put the Holy Spirit in His rightful place, at the apex!

Form Follows Function

To help understand the roles, I have bulleted several functions of each area. Try to commit to memory and often rehearse so that when you find yourself in a kingdom collision, you won't misdiagnose, rather respond accordingly.

The Spirit

- Born of God
- Relates directly to God
- Spirit to Spirit communication
- He is the director, the head, the apex
- Lacks nothing
- Same Spirit that raised Christ from the dead
- Accesses to the Master's mind

The Soul

- Subservient to the Spirit
- Made up of mind, will, and emotions.
- Thoughts, feelings, and desires.
- Deals in psychological areas of human
- Place where the choice resides
- A place whereby decisions are made
- Needs restoration
- Attention and focus reside

The Body

- Supports human systems of the body
- Uses physical senses
- The vehicle that houses two other components
- Subject to decay

The Fruition

Little children, you can be certain that you belong
to God and have conquered them, for the One who
is living in you is far greater than the one who is in
the world.

— 1 John 4:4, The Passion Translation

There is an adage among golfers stating that the "longest walk in
golf is from the practice ground to the playing ground." Meaning on the practice range, we often experience these moments of
euphoria where we can't miss a shot, demonstrating total command of the instrument. It feels like we cannot make a mistake
in these sessions. We convince ourselves that all is right in the
universe. We, golfers, get so excited, believing we have found
the proverbial secret to mastery. Unfortunately, as soon as we get
to the first hole, as soon as it matters, all is lost. We can't seem
to perform at all, and we now have this terrible feeling of being
totally out of control. Lost, frustrated, and wanting to quit, we
are despondent because nothing *transferred*.

In Christianity, a similar experience often takes place. It is
the *long walk* from Sunday to Monday. In service, we encounter the presence of the living God, and peace abounds. We are
washed by His words and experience profound joy. Our praise
exalts, and we are fixated on Jesus. The atmosphere is charged,
and then… we leave.

We return to everyday life, where we face Satan, his minions,
disobedient children, struggling marriages, corrupt politicians,
crime rates, and lack of funds. *Nothing seems to transfer.* We have
these inconsistent moments of highs on Sunday and emotionally
depleted lows by Wednesday.

Of course, this doesn't mean failure; after all, it is natural. Yet far too many continue in this cycle and are eventually frustrated at the lack of progression. Typically, a bad decision will follow. My hope is by being engaged in our actual reality and design, we recognize the genuine authority over the soul and the body, giving us the ability to materialize faith outcomes in the everyday.

How does this work? Let's look at marriage; for instance, when my wife and I find ourselves in a disagreement that is starting to get contentious, we will often say, "Wait, let's jump back into the kingdom." In other words, when we find ourselves NOT displaying the fruit of the Spirit, we go directly to the Spirit. We realize, "Hey, we are in our soul right now; let's allow God to run the show." Now we have transference and victory in a practical situation.

Fear is a massive influence in the world today, but I found it liberating once I understood a couple of fear facts. First, God didn't give fear to us, and second, fear is a function of my soul. Armed with that knowledge, I can accurately decipher the input and apply the Word accordingly.

Fasting is another great example. Why fast? Many good reasons, but a big one is that in "our weakness; He is strong."[91] A significant point of fasting is to deny the flesh and focus on the Spirit. My inner man seeks God, and the outer man submits. The pattern can be applied in any situation. Ever want to tell someone off, like really let them know how you feel? How about depression? Moments of feeling worthless. I am even suggesting that our design can play a role in sports.

Never compartmentalize; anytime your peace is disturbed, seek to understand the origin. Peace and joy live in His presence. If you're not zeroing in on His presence, then you're in the natural realm of your soul.

In my lifetime, I have found it difficult to trust. People who were very close to me, family, were involved in corrupted relationships. Sexual abuse, verbal abuse, and adultery were very prominent in my family lineage. It affected me.

I would be lying if I said I didn't have moments where I slipped into the realm of questioning myself and others close to me. During these moments of angst, I recognize that I am in the middle of a collision, and using the same formula, I administer His Word to my current encounter. That's the key.

Regardless of the situation or circumstance, knowing how we are constructed is crucial. There is so much freedom in the fact that now restored to our original creation; we are a functioning spirit being. We are no longer a dual entity; we are more than just a body led by assumptions and feelings.

By faith in Christ, the believer is quickened back to the *original architecture*. Those who have accepted Christ as their savior are born anew. The Spirit of God has resuscitated them in a fashion that coincides with the original intent of God's purpose.

When Christ took up residency, you became a living, walking, breathing tabernacle. Your body is a true temple of the Holy Spirit. It is pure God that is dwelling within.

CHAPTER 5

The Fifth Imperative: The Profession

A man's belly shall be satisfied with the fruit of his mouth; and with the increase of his lips shall he be filled. Death and life are in the power of the tongue: and they that love it shall eat the fruit thereof.

— Proverbs 18:20-21 NKJV

Performance Professions

The word profession means "an act of openly declaring or publicly claiming a belief, faith, or opinion."[92]

The Indicator

I told you that I was a golfer and a coach. Within the game, there is a numerical value known as a handicap. The handicap is an indicator of the proficiency level of a player; it is "a numerical measure of a golfer's *current playing status* used to enable players of varying abilities to compete against one another."[93] Along those lines, I believe Christians also have a method of measuring skill, thereby demonstrating a level of spiritual maturity; it is called the mouth.

What comes out of the mouth will indicate our belief system, signaling the plane on which we reside. So, to ensure we are taking successive steps, I have identified four essential elements that should be evident in our speech as God's children.

These elements are as follows:

- Creative speech
- Congruent speech
- Confrontational speech
- Complimentary speech

Creative Speech

Faith empowers us to see that the universe was created and beautifully coordinated by the power of God's words! He spoke, and the invisible realm gave birth to all that is seen.

— Hebrews 11:3, TPT

The first aspect is creative speech. God set a precedent on this all-important reality, and it's simple—our speech is creative. The heart believes, the mouth speaks, and things form. Know this powerful principle: "The physical realm was brought forth by the spiritual realm, not the other way around. Out of the mouth of God came spiritual seed-producing physical manifestation."[94] For example, when God said, "Let there be light,"[95] light was created.

Creative speaking is God's *modus operandi* for getting unseen things seen. As people created in His image, we should use the same template. Using our words in agreement with faith, we move from the conceptual to concrete. For everything that we see in our universe was founded upon the spoken word.

Did you know that in the New Testament, the word for seed is the Greek word *sperma*, which references something sown?[96] Seeds can be symbolic of our words, and the seeds you sow through speaking will germinate. Our speech will create life or death because the "seed produces after its own kind."[97]

My initiative is to assist you in making the *crucial nexus between speech and potential.*

The Power of Profession

My dear brothers and sisters, don't be so eager to become a teacher in the church since you know that we who teach are held to a higher standard of judgment. We all fail in many areas, but especially with our words. Yet if we're able to bridle the words we say, we are powerful enough to control ourselves in every way, and that means our character is mature and fully developed. Horses have bits and bridles in their mouths so that we can control and guide their large body. And the same with mighty ships, though they are massive and driven by fierce winds, yet they are steered by a tiny rudder at the direction of the person at the helm. And so the tongue is a small part of the body, yet it carries great power. Just think of how a small flame can set a huge forest ablaze.

— James 3:1-5, TPT

There is much to unpack here but let us focus on our primary message of reaching potential. In verse 4, one can see the tongue represents the ship's rudder. James tells us it is the small part of the ship that navigates the large part of the ship. He is showing us that just like the rudder, our tongues will direct. Since the mouth determines the course, words spoken and received have a mega impact on our fruitfulness. Words are not neutral; they will take us somewhere.

Agreement Verbalized Becomes the Word Materialized

Repeatedly, Scripture puts us on notice that what comes out of our mouth is a direct result of what we believe. Once in Christ, the condition of our lives and the level on which we operate, blessed, or cursed, is a direct result of essentially two items: *thought life and talk life.*

Our current realities are severely influenced by vocalizing the *demonic or the divine.* Marriage, relationships, finances, health, and most importantly, our spiritual well-being are a culmination of *our heart's beliefs and the utterances of those beliefs.* The mouth speaks what the heart believes, and the rudder does its job whether you are on the right course or not.

How Words Can Affect Us

Science backs up our Biblical claim of speech creativity. Check this out:

If I were to put you into an MRI scanner—a huge donut-shaped magnet that can take a video of the neural changes happening in your brain—flash the word "NO" for less than one second, you'd see a sudden release of dozens of stress-producing hormones and neurotransmitters. These chemicals immediately interrupt the normal functioning of your brain, impairing logic, reason, language processing, and communication. In fact, just seeing a list of negative words for a few seconds will make a highly anxious or depressed person feel worse, and the more you ruminate on them, the more you can actually damage key structures that regulate your memory, feelings, and emotions. [1] You'll disrupt your sleep, your appetite, and your ability to experience long-term happiness and satisfaction.

If you vocalize your negativity or even slightly frown when you say "no," more stress chemicals will be released, not only in your brain but in the listener's brain as well. [2] The listener will experience increased anxiety and irritability, thus undermining cooperation and trust. In fact, just hanging around negative people will make you more prejudiced toward others. [3]

Any form of negative rumination—for example, worrying about your financial future or health—will stimulate the release of destructive neurochemicals. And the same holds true for children: the more negative thoughts they have, the more likely they are to experience emotional turmoil. [4] But if you teach them to think positively, you can turn their lives around. [5][98]

It's a rather long quote, I get it, but look, the information and technology are finally catching up to the Bible. Today's scientific knowledge proves how the power of thought, expressed through the tongue, can create, and modify our brain function, affecting many of the physical aspects of the human system.

Congruent

With this next ingredient, I recommend making our speech harmonious with God's. The word congruent means "agreement or harmony."[99] Agreeing with the Holy Spirit is a fundamental characteristic of apex performers and should be expressed in our speech by *saying the same things that God says*, for that is the predominant meaning of the word *confession* in the New Testament.

You see, the Greek word *homologeo* means to confess, profess, or to "say the same thing as."[100] It is used this way more than twenty times in the New Covenant. The first time I heard it preached, I nearly fell off the pew. Why? I made the mistake of solely associating confession with admitting sin. Yes, this is a component of confession. However, by studying the words more carefully, I realized I missed a great opportunity to profess what God said, especially what He said about me.

As we speak aloud the harmonious tones of God's Word, we move towards an agreement with His will, His mind, and His purpose. Our words mobilize action, and we want that action to be discerned and directed by the Holy Ghost. Harmonious.

Confrontational

This next factor may sound surprising to you, but I am a firm believer that a significant aspect of our speech patterns should be confrontational. In the world today, we need to confront many thoughts, emotions, mindsets, and circumstances with God's authoritative power. Doing so can even save a life.

As mentioned earlier, I almost drowned in a riptide off the coast of Florida trying to help some young people. Things were dicey, and I came very close to losing my life. I know that God's grace and my ability to speak kept me alive. Fading fast and in real trouble, my first reaction was to pray. Next, my words turned very aggressive. I asked God for help, yes, of course, but I immediately kicked into a very determined mode that my biblical worldview trained me for. I told God that "I am not going out like this, not drowning, not with my wife and kids watching from the beach." I told Him, "This was not my destiny; this was not the plan, not how I was supposed to go."

I spoke Spirit to my mind, and *I confronted my crisis with Christ*. Telling myself to float,

I said to myself, "Tim if you panic, you die! You have to stay afloat." Rough waves were pummeling me at this point, and I was completely out of gas. I surfaced again when an orange buoy landed in front of my face. Barely able to hold on, the lifeguard crew got me onto the shore. Exhausted, I was carried from the water.

My thoughts and speech at that moment were very confrontational. Trust me; there was a definite divine collision that took place. I survived by relying on God to bring my natural facilities under submission and agree with His Word. God's prophetic words trumped my mind in the physical situation and saved my life.

As a result of this trauma, the experience is not easy to think about even to this day. When my mind begins to dwell on the *what-ifs*, a terrible feeling comes upon me; experts say this is a form of post-traumatic stress. Maybe so, but because of my renewed mind, my knowledge of Scripture, and my relationship with Jesus Christ, I know that I have the power and ability to decipher what is happening moment to moment. Again, I am experiencing an opportunity to apply the Word to my flesh. I recognize the collision. As a result, I can "change the channel" in my mind by confronting the natural realm with "*sperma.*" I don't have to succumb to the side effects of anxiety, for what is "born of God overcomes the world."[101]

Please do not misunderstand; I'm not advocating anyone avoid counseling or therapy. I just believe in true biblical and psychological balance. We have previously stated that physicians and counselors rarely, if ever, consider the spiritual aspect. Therefore, most traditional counseling (statistically provable) is unsuccessful mainly due to *cause and effect* discussed earlier in the book. Unfortunately, the "experts" deal mostly with symptoms, not causes.

Whether it is depression, fear, or a bad report, we, as disciples, have the ability and capacity to proclaim the Word of God.

Regardless of circumstances, we can choose to continually employ purposeful professions to ultimately force our bodies to line up. Abraham "considered not his own body,"[102] rather considered the Word of God and character more relevant than physical circumstance. He deemed God faithful and ultimately became a father as promised. His life's actions demonstrate to us, even today, that he relied more heavily on what God said rather than what his body told him. This technique is a prevalent thread throughout all Scripture.

The Selah

King David is an excellent example of one who made devout *confrontational professions*, producing victory in stressful scenarios. He would willingly devise faith-filled climates by speaking the truth of God's character. In addition, I believe he left us a *biblical blueprint* for victory couched in a mysterious phenomenon called a *selah*.

In several of the Psalms, depending on the version read, you will see the word *selah*. No one knows this word's exact definition or meaning, for it is difficult to define. Its origin is unknown, but most scholars believe it was some type of "pause or intermission."[103] However, in my worldview, it is an *intervention*.

King David was a master of flipping the script in tough times. Using the *selah*, he addressed the stress, changed the previous tone, and went directly to the Lord.

In the example below, pay close attention to the psychological demeanor of David before the *selah* and then look at his state after the pause. Take note of the pattern throughout the psalm. King David begins in one mode, downcast and downtrodden, then after the *selah/intervention*, comes out on the other side with a totally different attitude.

In describing Psalm 3, The Passion Translation's summary states, *"King David's song when he was forced to flee from Absalom, his own son The Humbling of a King."[104]*

Lord, I have so many enemies, so many who are against me. Listen to how they whisper their slander against me, saying: "Look. He's hopeless. Even God can't save him from this." Pause in his presence[a] (Selah) But in the depths of my heart I truly know that you, Yahweh, have become my Shield; You take me and surround me with yourself. Your glory covers me continually. You lift high my head when I bow low in shame. I have cried out to you, Yahweh, from your holy presence. You send me a Father's help.[105]

Like David, we too should *"pause in His presence"* and begin to reconcile God's Word and our feelings. Using a Bible-laced lexicon we can indeed change the course of our destiny.

David often felt incredible pressure as a leader, teacher, warrior, husband, father, and yes, even a sinner. Yet, he was a genius at reciting aloud God's Word, nature, and character. We should imitate.

Complimentary

> [8] This Book of the Law shall not depart from your mouth, but you shall meditate in it day and night, that you may observe to do according to all that is written in it. For then you will make your way prosperous, and then you will have good success.
>
> — Joshua 1:8, NKJV

The fourth component profession is what I call "complementary" speech. Now, I am not just talking about flattering or encouraging remarks. I'm referring to a little-known and under-taught Hebrew word that packs a significant punch.

It all stems from the accurate and complete definition of the word *meditate* in the Bible. The Hebrew word, *hagah*, means to murmur (in a positive manner), mutter, ruminate, and to say repeatedly.[106] In Greek, it means to "revolve in the mind."[107] The idea is that He wants us to cycle through His Word, continually professing His precious promises. We should do so aloud, for I like to say *"faith comes by hearing"[108] but goes forth by speaking.* Simply concentrate on His unshakable character and nature, then profess.

Biblical meditation is very different from Middle Eastern meditation, which is merely a neurological phenomenon creating a vacuum for the demonic. The Bible's version is the recycling of God's Word through repetition accompanied by images and pictures.

Hagah has a visualization element to its meaning, and for me, that realization was a game-changer. The visual component *compliments* the auditory element. As we verbalize the Word, we should complement the speech by picturing Christ. Combine your speech with imagining Christ with you in the moment. Put yourself in the situation with the King by your side and reflect.

Dr. Mark Virkler is a leading expert on Biblical meditation and has done groundbreaking research on the topic. The following is a quote from one of his great teachings:

> Spanish Old Testament scholar, Dr. Jesus Arambarri, did a careful syntactic and semantic study of the Hebrew verb hagah and the verbal phrase hagah, which is used in Joshua 1:8, and Psalm 1:2. He concluded that when the verb is used of the heart to denote meditating, it denotes "more than just speaking." Hebrew hagah is in Joshua 1:8 and Psalm 1:2 refers to a type of reflection that envisions or pictures God's deeds ("the envisioning [vergegenwärtigend] memory of Yahweh's acts of salvation"). Dr. Arambarri points to several other passages in the Hebrew Bible, besides Joshua 1:8 and Psalm 1:2, which prove that the Hebrew verb hagah meant not only to meditate verbally by "muttering" and "speaking," but also meant to "imagine," "devise (in the mind)," or "visualize/ visually ponder," in passages like Psalm 63:6; Prov. 24:2; Isa. 33:18.[109]

Did you catch the "more than just speaking" portion of that quote? Here is some more:

> This is why we conclude that practicing biblical meditation means visually pondering and picturing what God says is true in Scripture, while we keep the words of Scripture in our mouths, memorizing key passages. [110]
>
> Visualizing is not a New Age idea: it's a godly, heavenly idea that Satan stole and counterfeited. And the Hebrew hagah in Joshua 1:8 and Psalm 1:2 (and all the other passages in the Hebrew Bible where it is used) prove it. [111]
>
> — Dr. Mark Virkler

Coupling your speech with visualization, is a springboard, sending you straight to His presence where peace and joy reside.

Become Our Own EPA

In concluding this chapter, I wanted to share a final idea regarding faith professions. Preaching a sermon at White Dove Fellowship, I once heard Dr. Mike Millé state that "faith and fear come through the same ear." I could not agree with him more. Therefore, I find it necessary for us, as believers, to have a *technique* recognizing and applying all the elements above. That technique? We should become our own "EPA."[112]

The EPA "is a government agency created to protect human and environmental health." [113] Now, you may be thinking, *what in the helicopter does that have to do with Christianity?* My brothers and sisters, we have tendencies. One tendency is to pollute our atmosphere with the toxic waste of negative confessions coming

94   *The Sacred Seven*

from us or others. This cycle must be interrupted if we are going to reach our divine potential.

To protect your arena, each of us must begin to establish standards that prosper our environment, just like the EPA. Specifically, the EPA's role is to "**monitor** water quality, **identify** pollution problems and **develop** pollution control plans."[114]

MID

Borrowing from the three functions of the EPA, I put together an acronym to assist in the discernment of our private (what we say to ourselves) and public speech. It is very easy to remember and employ. As you become your own EPA, use the acronym **MID:**

- Monitor
- Identify
- Develop

Monitor

Christians should regularly monitor their speech. Monitoring—in the context of surveillance—"to listen to telephone calls, foreign radio broadcasts, etc. to find out information that might be useful;"[115] like a wiretap scenario in a movie, where the guys in the truck are hanging onto every word. As stated earlier, our words are clues. These clues tip us off to the condition of the heart.

In my line of work, I view myself as a professional listener. When people come in for a lesson, especially in the first lesson, I ask them a series of questions. These questions are specifically designed to elicit answers or responses that will help me decide what direction to take. For instance, I often ask them, "Do you like to practice?" If the player responds, "I don't practice much," that's going to tell me right away I will not be able to get too deep. I cannot reconstruct the swing if the person is not willing or unable to practice.

By asking these critical questions and monitoring the responses, I can *identify* specific problems and areas of need. The thoughts and beliefs spoken by the student give me a course of action as a coach. Our ability to listen to other people and ourselves will give us discernment to assist and assimilate. Christians should become professional listeners.

Identify

The next step is to identify the source. Locate the origin of what we are saying and make sure it agrees with God's Word. Ask yourself, "why do I believe this or why would I say such a thing?" Then do some investigation, filtering it with the truth of the gospel. It is of great benefit to view your words as feedback. The feedback will tell you if those thoughts are kingdom or cosmos.

Develop

The "D" is for the word develop. As spiritual beings with a voice, we need to *develop* and use a vocabulary based on a renewed heart aligned with the Bible.

As stated previously, words are like seeds, and the environment you plant them in is your life. Your life is the soil. The seeds are either pestilential or prophetic, fostering a healthy harvest or encouraging contamination.

Our purposeful divine decrees can overcome toxic thoughts and feelings. They can reinvent and re-energize the atmosphere. Depression, anxiety, worry, fear, reinforced by perverted speech, are often the result of the soul not under the authority of Christ. Remember, it's important to accurately diagnose what's really happening.

I know that sometimes you don't feel like you are an overcomer, but the reality is God gave you the capacity at any time to change your atmosphere by speaking His anointed Word. Human beings were endowed with certain rights by the Creator. The question is, what are we creating? Are we creating death or life? We would be remiss not to employ some inspection of our beliefs and subsequent speech.

CHAPTER 6

The Sixth Imperative: The Perdition

Whoever makes a practice of sinning is of the devil,
for the devil has been sinning from the beginning.
The reason the Son of God appeared was to destroy
the works of the devil.

— 1 John 3:8, ESV

Dealing with The Demonic

One morning, I was at Starbucks with some family when we started to broach the topic of God and Satan. As we were leaving, I had a family member tell me he "felt I talked too much about the devil." He said I "gave him too much credit." Was he right? I don't think so. Here is why.

Formerly, I mentioned I had canvassed the gospels chapter by chapter a few years back. Simply focusing on Christ, I didn't read anything else.

My findings? Jesus Christ consistently dealt with the demonic. The devil and his minions are a substantial theme throughout Scripture. Did you know that approximately a quarter of Jesus' ministry recorded in the Gospels was related to the topic? If it is not important, then why so much coverage? If I give the devil too much due, why does John say it is "the reason Jesus came?"[116] I am not arguing it is the only reason, but how many times does it use that language in the Bible? Let me help you, not many.

Dealing with the demonic is vital, and you will be hard-pressed to find many books on maximizing performance discussing demonic influence. However, that's precisely the point. Ignorance of Satan's practices often creates a *hole in the hedge* that gives way to perverted persuasion. It is a simple formula; adversarial indifference lowers our defenses.

The Sway

We know that we are of God, and the whole world lies under the sway of the wicked one.

— 1 John 5:19, NKJV

Above, we have another incredible yet alarming piece of Scripture by the same author. A scripture that is proven more accurate with every passing day. I am not convinced that we understand the consequences of such a statement. Just think about the enormous implications of these incredible words and the net result.

Proverbs tells us that "as a man thinks in his heart, so is he,"[117] and the above verse states that all of us are or have been persuaded by perdition. Our thinking before meeting the Messiah has been warped and swayed. Do you think that has a chance at affecting our potential? Truthfully, it is impossible to teach or talk about performance or potential without dealing with the devil.

1 John 3:8 is a neon sign for us. Failure to address this subject in connection with destiny, potential, and performance is flat-out criminal.

Why? Because Satan has had the massive advantage of being the primary contributor to our thought life before we accepted Christ—to *sway* is to persuade. That is why I call *him the "Sway Maker."*

1 John 5:19 expresses, almost everything we have been subjected to and educated from has been infiltrated with persuasion from the patriarch of perdition. Unless you were "born saved," accepting Jesus in the womb (joke), you have been *swayed.* If you went to public school, you were *swayed.* Macro-evolution, mindfulness, pseudoscience, sex education, etc., are all part of the lesson plan to take you away from the God's ideal.

Sway Defined

The word sway has several meanings. I have listed a few, and they are powerful:

- To move side to side or back and forth
- An influence weight or authority that moves to one side
- Persuasion
- Rule, dominion, or control
- Direct by power or moral force, to govern
- To bend or to warp[118]

These definitions are incredible, right? If we are moving side to side or back and forth, we are not gaining any ground. There is no linear progression. There is no flow toward discipleship, maturity, and most importantly, Christ Jesus.

The Four Cs

My spiritual mentor, Pastor Mike Millé, would always remind the congregation of his classic four Cs. He would tell us that Christians make most life decisions based on coins, clocks, calendars, and circumstances. I remember how that made me feel. I was pricked in my heart to repent because even though I was a man of prayer and Bible reading, I was still making decisions based on human reason and logic independent of our ultimate guide. That, my friends, is the effect of being *swayed*, running on autopilot doing what we have always done.

As I aged, matured, and raised children, I learned another "C-word" added to Pastor's incredible message: *crowds*.

The prevailing voices coming from the masses will create extreme pressure to go away from God, especially when Christian kids go to public school. Peer pressure is rough. Our kids are in a system that is the opposite of what we are teaching them.

Crowds are influential and can be effective at keeping us from pursuing Christ. Remember the blind beggar? The crowd told him to stay quiet. If he had folded, he would not have his miraculous sight.

It should be easy to see how we have been shaped by the "five Cs." Most of which are rooted in soulish-based protocols passed down and transferred from satanic *sway*.

Although saved, and blood-washed we still employ these carnal components, like the rungs, in decision-making scaffolding. It is just a matter of time before it crumbles, for as it says in 1 Corinthians, "no other foundation can anyone lay."[119]

Prior to Christ, our own beliefs were adopted and adapted from others. Think about it; almost everything we know is borrowed from influential people in our lives. The downside? Most of what we adopted is installed from sway-based programs all around us. Programs inherited from peers, professors, parents, and priests are without question the most significant source from which we gather our worldviews, life philosophies, and viewpoints. Apart from God, those sources have been corrupted.

Look, don't get upset. I am not saying your parents or teachers are/were bad people. What I am saying is without the divine insight illuminating our minds to the truth, we will *nat-*

urally embrace erroneous messages, especially if they come from well-meaning loved ones with good intentions.

As we grow older, we adopt our belief system. Devoid of the Holy Spirit for discernment, we are like uncovered pots allowing anyone and anything to add poison to the cauldron.

Messages like "it is okay to have sex outside the marriage bed, as long as you love them" or "it's okay to look at another woman as long as you don't touch her" are immoral philosophies. Moral relativism, whereby everyone has their brand of truth, is the new normal. How about this one: "it's natural, so it is okay." Wait, what? My whole point is not every thought is natural.

Brethren, I am not recommending paranoia. I am simply making you aware that Satan and his cronies' corrupt thoughts and agendas that influence potential. Why do you think Paul says to take our thoughts "captive." [120]

DIS-EASE

When I was a child, my mother gave me a bit of matriarchal advice. She told me never to handle birds, saying, "Timmy, they carry many diseases." Little did she know that was some of the best spiritual advice I have ever received. What do I mean? The "birds of the air"[121] carry infected thoughts that can deposit in your mind. If the ideas are pondered unsupervised, chemicals will be released from the brain, causing dis-ease. That is slang for disease, another Mike Millé concept. The best way he phrased it was that negative thoughts would "cause your 'ease' to be dissed." Fear, worry, anxiety, a.k.a. *sway*, can make you sick, terminally. *Sway* is a trojan horse, searching and looking to infect.

From now on you and the woman will be enemies,
as will your offspring and hers. You will strike his
heel, but he will crush your head."

— Genesis 3:15, TLB

The Adversary

We must be on guard because Satan hates us. Why? Two reasons: first, God used people, in particular the Jewish people, to bring forth the Redeemer. Second, God is using humanity to share His kingdom plan. Scripture records Satan's focus was to stop the coming Messiah before the cross. Since Calvary, Satan adjusted his agenda to hinder you and me from manifesting the Messiah!

… lest Satan should take advantage of us; for we are
not ignorant of his devices.

— 2 Corinthians 2:11, NKJV

He comes to "steal, kill, and destroy."[122] He is the "father of lies." [123] He wants you to fail, and he impregnates your mind with thoughts. He tempts and manipulates others to distract you from your mission. I learned from Dr. Millé when he taught me early on that "behind every personality; there is a principality." Make no mistake; his job is to destroy you and your witness.

The good news is we possess the ability to repent and make a conscious choice to get into God's Word and perform some reconnaissance on our enemy so as not to suffer the consequences.

CHAPTER 7

The Seventh Imperative: The Pivot

His message was this: "At last the fulfillment of the age has come. It is time for the realm of God's kingdom to be experienced in its fullness. Turn your lives back to God and put your trust in the hope-filled gospel!"

— Mark 1:15 (TPT)

Now how do we pull all this information together and advance towards our kingdom potential? Simple: repentance. Unfortunately, many children of God have an incomplete and misguided view of repentance. This flawed perspective misses an opportunity to employ the Holy Spirit, the ultimate life strategist I liken to a *Turnaround Specialist*.

The Turnaround Specialist

I am a big fan of ultra-successful business consultant and author Brian Tracy. In his bestselling book *Turbo Strategy,* he informs his readers how corporations change direction when badly underperforming. He proceeds to explain how the companies will often rely on what is known as a *turnaround specialist.* What exactly is a turnaround specialist? Mr. Tracy explained it this way:

Often, when a company gets into trouble, the board or company owners bring in a turnaround specialist and put that person in charge. The reason they do this is because the turnaround specialist has no vested interest in anything that has happened up to that moment. The turnaround specialist draws a line under the past and focuses totally on the future and the survival of the business. You need to do the same.[124]

— Brian Tracy

To make sure we have a complete understanding, let's look at another great explanation:

One of the biggest benefits of hiring a turnaround expert is objectivity; he or she will bring a fresh set of eyes and perspective that an employee can't provide. With this objectivism, the specialist can make unpopular recommendations and decisions that, while difficult, are in the best interest of the company.[125]

— Don Sadler

This language immediately grabbed my attention. It was so exciting to learn about the qualities of the *turnaround*. I could not get over the fact that secular companies would employ one of the most biblical strategies in the Word of God. Repentance!

Biblical Repentance Defined

What is the first thing that comes to mind when you hear the word repent? What does that look like? My concern is most of us could not define the term correctly. Additionally, it is my experience that far too often, repentance has been associated solely with sin. Well, that is an incomplete and inaccurate stereotype. I am not alone in this assessment. Look at what the great pastor and author from California, Rick Warren, has to say:

> The renewal of your mind is related to the word "repentance." I know repentance is a dirty word for a lot of people. They think it means something bad, something they don't really want to do, something painful. They think of a guy standing on a street corner with a sign that says, "Repent! The world's about to end!" Repentance has nothing to do with your behavior. It is about changing your mind, learning to think differently. "Repent" means to make a mental U-turn. It's something you do in your mind, not with your behavior. Changing the way you think will then affect your emotions and affect your behavior.[126]

> — Rick Warren

I agree with Pastor Warren. When people think about repentance, they tend to link it solely with punishment. This incomplete association could lead to guilt, shame, and frustration in the body. Not seeing the whole picture pertaining to repentance could cause some to avoid God's presence, which we know is disastrous. You do not have to torture yourself or do something painful to "make up for your wrong-doings." All you need to do is change your mind.

Repentance is defined in both New Testament Greek and Old Testament Hebrew. In the Hebrew language, repentance means to "turn back"[127] and go in the opposite direction. In

Greek, it means "to think differently."[128] So, let's pair them up together to get the whole meaning.

To repent is to make a new decision and go in another direction. It is that simple. Here is more from Pastor Warren on the subject:

> When I repent, I make a mental U-turn. I turn from guilt to forgiveness. I turn from purposelessness to purpose in life. I turn from no hope to new hope. I turn from frustration to freedom. I turn from darkness to light. I turn from hell to heaven. I turn from hatred to love. I also changed the way that I think about God. He's not mad at me; I'm deeply flawed, but I'm deeply loved. I change the way I think about you, I change the way I think about my kids, and I change the way I think about my wife. I change the way I think about the world, I change the way I think about the economy, and I change the way I think about my past, my present, and my future.[129]

That, my friends, is a *turnaround*.

Look Ahead

As if that wasn't enough, how freeing it is for the believer to know that the *turnaround* is no longer interested in our previous rebellious resume. Brian Tracy made a very Christlike statement regarding how the *turnaround* begins to guide the underperforming. The *turnaround*, like Christ, "draws a line under the past."[130] This phraseology is business jargon for putting the past behind and focusing solely on what's ahead. The same is true with Christ. The Spirit is no longer focused on the past behavior, for He "drew the line" at the new birth. Intently, He now focuses on our future role as apex performers in the ecosystem assigned.

Pivoting to High Performance

In my performance worldview, repenting is all about pivoting. Our decision to spin at the prompting of the Holy Spirit is the mechanism for apex performers to reach our kingdom potential. Habitually, we should seek out opportunities in our private time to pivot towards godly perspectives and become adept at "strategy exchange."

At the new birth, we repent for our rebellion against a suffering savior. Afterward, we commit to reconciling God's Word with every area and aspect of our life. As we find areas not aligned with God's Word, we exchange our views for His and do a 180, an about-face. This ability to recognize and turn your thought life and actions towards God's Word is a tremendous factor in our journey towards kingdom potential. Yet, there is also an incredible side benefit. As we traverse our kingdom journey, we start to see repentance as a fantastic gift, a weapon of mass destruction to the carnal nature. We are pivoting away from the *sway* and stockpiling revelation to be employed throughout the course of our lives. Biblical inventory is now at our disposal to be deployed in all situations, regardless of circumstance.

High-performing Christians rely on the Holy Spirit, who is the turning tide in the believer's life. We thrive as we place Him in charge of running the whole proverbial show. Like those fortune 500 companies, Christians should practice total reliance and exude compliance. We must do what the Turnaround commands.

TIM BROWN

The Process

"Repentance represents the acquisition of a Biblical worldview over a period of time." [131]

It takes time to cultivate the skill; the more you practice, the more you see the fruit, but remember, time is still an element. Christianity, like golf, is a process. Jesus said to his disciples, "Follow me, and I will make you to become." [132] Making you become something doesn't happen all at once; His very language denotes a process. Positionally, we are made brand new, yes, but the "renewing of the mind" occurs intentionally and over time as we download the truth.

That is one reason I strongly emphasize not condemning others. The truth is that we don't know where people are in the process. As stated, earlier in the book, it is one thing to discern what comes out of a person's mouth, and I think it is reasonable to examine the fruit of someone's life. But we must be careful not to damage potential. I'm not excusing the sin, but it was not until I adopted Christ's perspective on topics such as sex, marriage, and finances that I changed my behavior, I pivoted.

For example, a few years into my walk, I did a complete 180 about tithing. My wife and I read, prayed, and started trusting God with our finances. We looked at what the Bible said compared to what we were doing and decided to "pivot" and go in another direction. God designed the operation to work that way. Let me ask, what have you exchanged since becoming a person of faith?

My advice is never to stop making that biblical "U-turn." As one continues digging in the scriptures, the Turnaround will highlight areas, not in harmony with the Messiah's. It is a work to be accomplished moment-to-moment, twenty-four-seven, three hundred and sixty-five. As the Holy Spirit leads us, mastering the flexibility to pivot and walk in a new direction is the essence of the Christian's ability to produce fruit.

"Most of us go through life not recognizing that our worldviews have been deeply affected by the world. Through the media and other influences, the secularized American view of history, law, politics, science, God, and man affects our thinking more than we realize. We then are "taken captive through hollow and deceptive philosophy, which depends on human tradition and the basic principles of this world rather than on Christ.[133]

— Colossians 2:8

What Repentance Is Not

Quickly, I want to touch on another misunderstood element of repentance: emotional reactions. In fact, Derek Prince gave a strong caution regarding this when he stated that "strong emotion is not necessarily proof of repentance."[134] Feelings can be fickle. Emotions can accompany true repentance but are not necessarily proof of a changed mind. Moreover, repentance is not the same as worldly sorrow. Remorse is different from repentance. *We can feel strong remorse without changing course.* That is not true repentance.

Repentance is the act of literally pivoting from our old ways and taking successive steps towards a Christ-like attitude and actions. Repentance is more than feeling guilty or ashamed. Repentance is recognizing we are out of alignment in a specific area and making up our mind to do something about it.

Repentance Is Primary

From then on, Jesus began to preach, "Repent of
your sins and turn to God, for the Kingdom of
Heaven is near."

— Matthew 4:17, NLT

Repentance is primary. Search the scriptures. Repentance is a
priority with God and necessary to experience our apical potential. Our God is a God of love, grace, mercy, and don't miss
this one, order. He often works sequentially. Repentance was
the *first* message Christ preached after the temptation, and it was
the significant tone from John the Baptist. The words of Christ
uttered on the record after the wilderness experience were as
follows: "repent and believe. "[135] Why? God is into priority. First,
He wants the relationship restored. Second, He desires kingdom
thinking. Then comes the conduct which yields kingdom fruit.

Prove by the way you live that you have repented of
your sins and turned to God.

— Matthew 3:8, NLT

Repentance is the foundation upon which the entire apex
performance system is built. It is one of the most valuable and
incredible gifts given to us by our Lord. Pivoting back towards
Him will have a profound and direct effect on our destiny. Like
the prodigal who "came to himself, "[136] we must immediately
react to any hint of the turnaround's mercy and grace. Never
gamble with a kingdom moment. Recognize what is happening
and turn. Enlist the Turnaround's assistance, and we will begin
to walk with our faces now toward Him and not away from Him.

Finally, I hope you have enjoyed a challenging yet unique outlook on realizing your potential. I pray now that you set out to *exhibit* God's touch on your life, displaying his power in your ecosystem "by the way you live."

NOTES AND REFERENCE

1   Biologyonline.com, https://www.biologyonline.com/dictionary/trophic-dynamics, March 2021.

2   Colin Dunn, "Importance of Apex Predators in a Healthy Ecosystem," https://greenerideal.com/news/environment/7066-the-importance-of-apex predators/June 10, 2011.

3   Colin Dunn, "Importance of Apex Predator," https://greenerideal.com/news/environment/7066-the-importance-of-apex predators/June 10, 2011.

4   "Progenitor," Dictionary.com, https://www.dictionary.com/browse/progenitor, 2019.

5   Bill Johnson (@BillJohnsonMinistries), "Royalty is my identity; Servanthood is my assignment; Intimacy with God is my life source," Facebook, post, 9/13/2015, https://www.facebook.com/BillJohnsonMinistries/posts/royalty-is-my-identity-servanthood-is-my-assignment-intimacy-with-god-is-my-life/10153449288793387/.

6   John 3:16, NKJV.

7   Paul Yonggi Cho, *Revelation* (Lake Mary, FL: Creation House, 1991), 20.

8   "Compensation," Dictionary.com, https://www.dictionary.com/browse/compensation, 2016.

9   Andy Stanley, *VISIONEERING – A Seven Day Devotional by Andy Stanley,* You Version Bible app, Colorado Springs, Colorado, Multnomah, 2005.

10   Andy Stanley, *VISIONEERING – A Seven Day Devotional by Andy Stanley*, You Version Bible app, Colorado Springs, Colorado, Multnomah, 2005.

11   Derek Prince, "The Delusion of Independence," derekprince.com, 2018, nhttps://www.derekprince.com/teaching/98-2.

12   Matthew Henry, "Luke 15 Bible Commentary", christianity.com, https://www.christianity.com/bible/commentary.php?com=mh&b=42&c=15.

13   James Strong, "kollaó," *Strong's Exhaustive Concordance of the Bible* (Thomas Nelson Publishers, Nashville, Tennessee, 1990), G2853, 43.

14   Pastor Bob Koeling, "Sermon - The Prodigal Son," (First Assembly of God, 2002).

15   Mary Bradbury Jones, "Productivity Tip: Finding the Lead Domino," August 26, 2015, https://climb.pcc.edu/blog/productivity-tip-finding-the-lead-domino.

16   Matthew 8:10, KJV.

17   Matthew Henry, "Matthew Henry's Commentary," biblehub.com, 2018.

18   Del Tackett, "Why Is a Christian Worldview Important?", Focus on the Family, January 2010, https://www.focusonthefamily.com/parenting/why-is-a-christian-worldview-important/.

19   Judson Cornwall, *Worship As David Lived It* (Revival Press, Shippensburg, PA 1990), 6.

20   Finis J. Dake, *Dake Annotated Reference Study Bible* (Lawrenceville, GA, 1991),122.

21 Oswald Chambers, "The Habit of rising to the Occasion," in *My Utmost for His Highest,* (Barbour Publishing, Inc. Ohio, 1935), n.pag.

22 "Calling," Merriam Webster, https://www.merriam-webster.com/dictionary/calling, 2019.

23 "Exhibit," Dictionary.com, https://www.dictionary.com/browse/exhibit, 2021.

24 Matthew 5:13, NKJV.

25 Matthew 5:14, NKJV.

26 Matthew 4:19, NKJV.

27 Colossians 1:10, NKJV.

28 John 15:5, NKJV.

29 Ephesians 2:10 NKJV

30 Andy Stanley, *VISIONEERING – A Seven Day Devotional by Andy Stanley,* You Version Bible app, Colorado Springs, CO, Multnomah, 2005.

31 Andy Stanley, *VISIONEERING – A Seven Day Devotional by Andy Stanley*, You Version Bible app, Colorado Springs, CO, Multnomah, 2005.

32 Psalm 23:5, NKJV.

33 A.W. Tozer, *The Pursuit of God* (Christian Publications, Camp Hill PA, 1982),64.

34 Matthew 5:16, *Verse-by-Verse Bible*, StudyLight.org. https://www.studylight.org/commentary/matthew/5-16.html.accessed 2018

35 Albert Barnes, "Barnes' Notes," biblehub.com, https://biblehub.com/commentaries/barnes/matthew/5.htm. Accessed 2018

36   Pastor Mike Millé, White Dove Fellowship, 2006 accessed 2006.

37   Gary Chapman, "The Five Love Languages," lifeway.com, https://www.lifeway.com/en/articles/thanksgiving-languages-of-gratitude. Accessed 2019.

38   A.W. Tozer, *The Pursuit of God* (Christian Publications, Camp Hill PA, 1982), 127.

39   "Modify," The Free Dictionary, https://www.thefreedictionary.com/modify. Accessed 2019.

40   "Performance," The Free Dictionary, https://www.thefreedictionary.com/performance. Accessed 2019.

41   "So as to," The Free Dictionary, https://www.thefreedictionary.com/so+as+to. Accessed 2019.

42   Bruce Wilkinson, *Secrets of the Vine*, (Multnomah Publisher Inc, Sisters, Oregon, 2001) 2008

43   Matthew 5:14, ESV.

44   Judson Cornwall, *Worship As David Lived It* (Revival Press, Shippensburg, PA 1990), 83.

45   Andrew Murray, *The Blood of Jesus* (Whitaker House, PA, 1993), 108.

46   Matthew 28:19, NKJV

47   Colin Dunn, "Importance of Apex Predators for a Healthy Ecosystem," https://greenerideal.com/news/environment/7066-the-importance-of-apex-predators, June 10, 2011. Accessed 2018.

48   Matthew Henry, "Matthew Henry's Commentary on the Whole," biblehub.com, https://biblehub.com/commentaries/mhcw/2_thessalonians/1.htm. Accessed 2019

49 Finis J. Dake, *Dake Annotated Reference Bible* (Lawrenceville, GA, 1991), 226.

50 Titleist, "The Moment of Impact. An Inside Look at Titleist Golf Ball R&D," Titleist, video, 2013, 3:50, https://www.youtube.com/watch?v=6TA1s1oNpbk. 2018.

51 Titleist, "The Moment of Impact. An Inside Look at Titleist Golf Ball R&D," Titleist, video, 2013, 3:50, https://www.youtube.com/watch?v=6TA1s1oNpbk. 2018.

52 Derek Prince, "Authority and Power of God's Word," Derek Prince Ministries, video, 23 September 2020, 1:00:32, https://www.youtube.com/watch?v=BU8G-4JG7F8M. 2020.

53 Colossians 1:10, ESV.

54 1 John 14:4, NKJV.

55 1 John 5:4, NKJV.

56 2 Corinthians 10:5, NIV.

57 Romans 12:2, KJV.

58 Mike Hebron, used with permission. 2000.

59 Titleist, "The Moment of Impact. An Inside Look at Titleist Golf Ball R&D," Titleist, video, 2013, 3:50, https://www.youtube.com/watch?v=6TA1s1oNpbk. 2018.

60 "Mastery," Merriam Webster, https://www.merriam-webster.com/dictionary/mastery. 2019.

61 "Wield," Vocabulary.Com, https://www.vocabulary.com/dictionary/wield. 2019.

62 Ezra 7:6, ESV.

63 Ezra 7:25, ESV.

64　"Eye-hand coordination," The Free Dictionary, https://medical-dictionary.thefreedictionary.com/eye-hand+coordination, Retrieved September 14, 2021.

65　Ephesians 1:18, KJV.

66　Matthew 6:22, KJV.

67　George Barna, *Think Like Jesus* (Integrity Publishing, Nashville, 2003), 23.

68　George Barna, *Think Like Jesus* (Integrity Publishing, Nashville, 2003), 21.

69　George Barna, *Think Like Jesus* (Integrity Publishing, Nashville, 2003), 21.

70　George Barna, *Think Like Jesus* (Integrity Publishing, Nashville, 2003), 23.

71　George Barna, *Think Like Jesus* (Integrity Publishing, Nashville, 2003), 23.

72　Homer Kelley, The Golfing Machine (Star System Press, Seattle, 1969), VII.

73　1 John 4:4, NKJV.

74　Romans 8:11, NLT.

75　Ephesians 2:8-9, NKJV.

76　1 Corinthians 2:16, NKJV.

77　1 John 2:20, NKJV.

78　Jeremiah 29:11, NKJV.

79　Proverbs 18:21, NKJV.

80　2 Corinthians 4:4 NKJV.

81　"Outside Agency," Dictionary. University, https://dictionary.university/outside%20agency. Accessed 2021.

82 Oswald Chambers, "Quote," https://utmost.org/quotes/2371/. Accessed 2021.

83 Oswald Chambers, "Don't Plan Without God," https://utmost.org/don%E2%80%99t-plan-without-god/. Accessed 2021

84 Andy Stanley, *VISIONEERING – A Seven Day Devotional by Andy Stanley*, You Version Bible app, Colorado Springs, Colorado, Multnomah, 2005. 2019

85 Oswald Chambers, "The Divine Commandment of Life," https://utmost.org/the-divine-commandment-of-life/2018. Accessed 2021.

86 Derek Prince, "Spirit, Soul and Body," https://www.derekprince.com/teaching/96-2. Accessed 2017.

87 Watchman Nee, *The Release of the Spirit* (Christian Fellowship Publishers, New York, 2000), 12.

88 Watchman Nee *The Release of the Spirit* (Christian Fellowship Publishers, New York, 2000), Introduction.

89 Derek Prince, "Are You Spiritual or Soulish," https://www.derekprince.com/teaching/96-3. Accessed 2017.

90 Genesis 1:11, KJV.

91 2 Corinthians 12:8-10, KJV.

92 "Profession," Merriam-Webster, https://www.merriam-webster.com/dictionary/profession, Accessed 2019.

93 "Handicap (golf)," last modified 13 October 2021, https://en.wikipedia.org/wiki/Golf_handicap. Accessed 2018

94 John Osteen, *The Power of Your Words*, Keith Alan, video, 28:26, https://www.youtube.com/watch?v=nnV6QdArW6c,1988. Accessed 2018.

95   Genesis 1:3, KJV.

96   "Sperma," James Strong, *Strong's Exhaustive Concordance of the Bible* (Thomas Nelson Publishers, Nashville, Tennessee, 1990), G4690, 66.

97   Genesis 1:11, KJV.

98   Andrew Newberg and Mark Waldman, "Why This Word Is So Dangerous to Say or Hear," Psychology Today, 1 Aug. 2012, https://www.psychologytoday.com/us/blog/words-can-change-your-brain/201208/why-word-is-so-dangerous-say-or-hear. Accessed 2019

99   "Congruent," Vocabulary.Com, https://www.vocabulary.com/dictionary/congruent, Accessed 2019.

100   "homologeo," biblestudytools.com, https://www.biblestudytools.com/lexicons/greek/kjv/homologeo.html accessed 2019

101   1 John 5:4, NIV.

102   Romans 4:19 KJV.

103   Penny Noyes, "What Does Selah Mean in the Bible," christianity.com, https://www.christianity.com/wiki/christian-terms/what-does-selah-mean-in-the-bible.html, Accessed April 2019.

104   Psalm 3, TPT.

105   Pslam 3:1-3, TPT.

106   James Strong, *Strong's Exhaustive Concordance of the Bible* (Thomas Nelson Publishers, Nashville, Tennessee, 1990), H1897, 32. 2019.

107   Madeline Pena, "Christian Disciplines," justdisciples.com, https://justdisciple.com/christian-meditation. Accessed 2021.

108 Romans 10:17, NKJV.

109 Dr. Mark Virkler, "Communion with God," April 2012, https://www.cwgministries.org/blogs/biblical-meditation-involves-imagination. Accessed 2015.

110 Dr. Mark Virkler, "Communion with God," April 2012, https://www.cwgministries.org/blogs/biblical-meditation-involves-imagination. Accessed 2015.

111 Dr. Mark Virkler, "Communion with God," April 2012, https://www.cwgministries.org/blogs/biblical-meditation-involves-imagination. Accessed 2015.

112 "Our Mission and What We Do," EPA, https://www.epa.gov/aboutepa/our-mission-and-what-we-do, Accessed August 5, 2018.

113 "Our Mission and What We Do," EPA, https://www.epa.gov/aboutepa/our-mission-and-what-we-do, Accessed August 5, 2018.

114 "Our Mission and What We Do," EPA, https://www.epa.gov/aboutepa/our-mission-and-what-we-do, Accessed August 5, 2018.

115 "Monitor," Oxford Learners' Dictionary, https://www.oxfordlearnersdictionaries.com/us/definition/american_english/monitor_2, Accessed 2020.

116 1 John 3:8, ESV.

117 Proverbs 23:7, NKJV.

118 "Sway," Wiktionary, https://en.wiktionary.org/wiki/sway, Accessed 2019.

119 1 Corinthians 3:11, NKJV.

120 2 Corinthians 10:5, NIV.

121 Matthew 8:20, KJV.

122 John 10:10, KJV.

123 John 8:44, New Life Version

124 Brian Tracy, *TurboStrategy: 21 Powerful Ways to Transform Your Business* (Amacom, 2003), 22.

125 Don Sadler, "Hiring a Turnaround Specialist," all-Business, https://www.allbusiness.com/hiring-a-turn-around-specialist-13935088-1.html, Accessed 2021.

126 Rick Warren, "If You Want to Change, Start with Your Thinking," https://pastorrick.com/if-you-want-to-change-start-with-your-thinking-2/. Accessed 2021

127 "Shuwb,", https://www.biblestudytools.com/lexicons/hebrew/nas/shuwb.html.

128 "Metanoeo," James Strong, Strong's Exhaustive Concordance of the Bible, (Thomas Nelson Publishers, Nashville, Tennessee, 1990), G3340, 47

129 Rick Warren, "What You Think You Are," https://pastorrick.com/what-you-think-you-are%20/. Accessed 2020.

130 Brian Tracy, *TurboStrategy: 21 Powerful Ways to Transform Your BusinessC*, (Amacom, 2003), 22.

131 Tackett Del, "Why Is a Christian Worldview Important?" Jan 2010, https://www.focusonthefamily.com/parenting/why-is-a-christian-worldview-important/.

132 Mark 1:17, ESV.

133 Tackett Del, "Why Is a Christian Worldview Important?", Jan 2010, https://www.focusonthefamily.com/parenting/why-is-a-christian-worldview-important/. Accessed 2021

134 Derek Prince, *The Spirit Filled Believers Handbook* (Creation House, Lake Mary Florida, 1993), 119.

135 Mark 1:15, ESV.

136 Luke 15:17, NKJV.

CPSIA information can be obtained
at www.ICGtesting.com
Printed in the USA
LVHW041653300322
714805LV00007B/173